FINANCES AND YOU

Finances and You

A Beginners Guide to Understanding Finance

CHARLES TOMLINSON

Bubba's Publishing House LLC

Contents

First Printing, 2021

To my wife, for whom this wouldn't be possible without.

Disclaimer

The advice and strategies found within may not be suitable for every situation. This work is sold with the understanding that neither the author nor the publisher are held responsible for the results accrued from the advice in this book. The information presented here is for informational and educational purposes only. It does not construe financial or tax advice. The ideas and strategies should never be used without first assessing your own personal and financial situation, or without consulting financial professional. You assume the sole responsibility of relying on this information at your own risk and we do not endorse any companies or products offered here. Past performance is commonly used in investment and financial books/markets/websites where there are unpredictable and ever-changing results and outcomes.

Chapter 1

INTRODUCTION TO FINANCE

The word "finance" refers to a wide range of activities including banking, debit, credit, capital markets, money, and investments. Finance, in its most basic form, refers to money management and the method of obtaining necessary funds. Cash, banking, credit, deposits, properties, and liabilities are all part of financial structures, and finance is responsible for overseeing, creating, and studying them.

Microeconomic and macroeconomic theories are responsible for many of the fundamental principles of finance. The time value of money is one of the most fundamental theories. It claims that a dollar today is worth more than a dollar in the future.

Essential Takeaways

Banking, leverage or debt, credit, capital markets, money, savings, and the development and regulation of financial structures are all covered by finance.

Microeconomic and macroeconomic theories underpin basic financial principles.

Personal finance, corporate finance, and public (government) finance are the three major subcategories of finance.

The mechanisms through which customers and companies obtain financial products are known as financial services. The financial services sector is a major contributor to a country's GDP.

Financing Forms

The finance sector includes three major subcategories: personal finance, corporate finance, and public (government) finance, since individuals, corporations, and government agencies all need funding to function.

Finances for Individuals

Financial planning entails assessing an individual's current financial situation to develop plans for potential needs while staying within budget constraints. Personal finance is unique to each person's situation and activities. As a result, financial plans are heavily influenced by a person's earnings, living needs, ambitions, and desires.

Individuals must, for example, save for retirement, which necessitates saving or investing sufficient funds during their working lives to fund their long-term goals. Personal finance encompasses this form of financial management decision.

Purchases of financial goods such as credit cards, insurance, mortgages, and different forms of savings are all part of personal finance. Individuals use checking and savings accounts, as well as online and mobile payment systems like PayPal and Venmo, which are all considered part of personal finance.

Investing

Finance for Corporations

Corporate finance refers to the financial operations that go into running a company, with a division or department in charge of overseeing those activities.

A large corporation can need to determine whether to raise additional funds through a bond issue or a stock sale. Investment banks can advise the company on certain matters and assist in the marketing of securities.

Angel investors and venture capitalists can provide funding in return for a percentage of ownership in a startup. If a business succeeds and chooses to go public, it will sell stock on a stock exchange in an initial public offering (IPO).

In other instances, a business may be attempting to budget its capital and determine which projects to fund and which to postpone to expand. Corporate finance encompasses both of these kinds of decisions.

Finances of the State

Taxation, borrowing, budgeting, and debt-issuance strategies are all aspects of public finance that influence how a government pays for the services it provides to the public.

Through controlling capital allocation, income distribution, and economic stability, the federal government helps to prevent market failure. Taxation is the primary source of regular funding. Borrowing money from banks, insurance companies, and other countries is also a way for the government to fund its spending.

A government agency has social and fiscal responsibilities in addition to managing resources in day-to-day operations. A government is required to provide sufficient social services for its tax-paying citizens as well as sustain a stable economy, allowing people to save and keep their money healthy.

Services in the Financial Sector

The mechanisms through which customers and companies obtain financial products are known as financial services. The financial service provided by a payment system provider as it accepts and transfers funds between payers and recipients is a simple example. Accounts settled by check, credit and debit cards, and electronic funds transfer are included.

The terms "financial services" and "financial products" are not interchangeable. Mortgages, securities, shares, and insurance plans are examples of financial goods; financial services are activities provided by a financial planner to a client such as investment advice and management.

One of the most important sectors of the economy is financial services. It is the engine that drives a country's economy, allowing for the free movement of capital and liquidity in the marketplace. Banks, investment houses, financing agencies, insurance companies, insurers, accounting services, and real estate brokers are among the financial firms that make up the industry.

Consumer trust and purchasing power are improved when this sector and a country's economy are high. When the financial services industry struggles, the economy suffers and a recession ensues.

What are the Different Types of Financial Activities?

Financial operations are the acts and transactions taken by corporations, governments, and individuals to achieve their economic objectives. They are financial operations that include money inflows and outflows. Buying and selling goods (or assets), issuing stocks, initiating loans, and maintaining accounts are just a few examples.

Both the sale of stock and the repayment of debt are financial operations for a business. Individuals and states, likewise, engage in financial practices such as taking out loans and levying taxes to achieve particular monetary goals.

An Overview of Finance vs. Economics

Economics and finance are intertwined and educate and influence each other, even though they are mostly taught and viewed as separate disciplines. These studies are important to investors because they have a significant impact on the markets. Investors must resist "either/or" debates when it comes to economics and finance; both are necessary and useful.

The emphasis of economics as a general social science is more on the big picture or general questions regarding human actions about the distribution of real resources. Finance is more concerned with money management strategies and tools. Both economics and finance are concerned with how businesses and investors assess risk and return. Historically, economics has been more theoretical and finance has been more realistic, but the distinction has become much less pronounced in the last 20 years.

In reality, the two fields seem to be merging in certain ways. Governments, companies, and capital markets all employ economists and finance practitioners. There will always be a separation at some fundamental stage, but both are likely to remain vital to the economy, investors, and markets for many years to come.

Essential Takeaways

Even if the particulars are different, economics and finance are interrelated disciplines that teach each other.

Finance is an economics-based discipline that examines liquidity, banking, credit, investments, and other aspects of the financial system.

Public finance, corporate finance, and personal finance are three subcategories of finance that are related but distinct.

Economics examines how products and services are produced, distributed, and consumed, as well as how the economy as whole works and the people who drive economic activity.

Macroeconomics, which studies the entire economy, and microeconomics, which studies basic factors within the economy, are the two major divisions of economics.

Investing

In certain ways, finance is a subset of economics. Finance refers to the management, development, and analysis of money, banking, credit, investments, properties, and liabilities, as well as the study of financial instruments that make up financial structures. Public finance, corporate finance, and personal finance are the three types of finance.

The study of prices, interest rates, money flows, and financial markets are traditionally the subject of finance. Finance, in a broader sense, is concerned with issues such as the time value of assets, rates of return, cost of capital, optimal financial structures, and risk quantification.

Finance, or corporate finance, entails controlling a company's assets, liabilities, profits, and debt. Businesses may get money in several ways, including equity investments and credit agreements. A business might take out a bank loan or set up a line of credit—acquiring and managing debt effectively will help a company grow and become more profitable.

Personal finance refers to any of an individual's or household's financial choices and practices, such as budgeting, insurance, mortgage planning, investments, and retirement planning.

Tax structures, government spending, budget procedures, stabilization strategy and tools, debt issues, and other government considerations are all covered by public finance.

Particular Points to Consider

Many people who work on Wall Street as analysts, brokers, or fund managers have a finance degree as a common denominator. Similarly, several people who work for commercial banks, insurance firms, and other financial service providers have finance degrees. A finance degree may lead to senior management positions in companies and businesses outside of the finance industry.

Finance entails determining the fair value of a variety of financial instruments, such as determining the fair value of a variety of investment goods. Stock-price models like the capital asset pricing model (CAPM) and choice models like Black-Scholes are used in finance. Finance often entails deciding a corporation's best dividend or debt policy, as well as an investor's best asset allocation strategy.

Finance, it could be argued, affects the markets by releasing a seemingly endless stream of new goods. Even though many derivatives and advanced financial products were vilified in the aftermath of the Great Recession, many of these instruments were created to meet and solve consumer demands and needs. Derivatives, for example, may be used to shield the financial system from harm in the event of a recession by hedging risk for investors, hedge funds, or large banks.

Finance is more applied, whereas economics is more theoretical; nevertheless, both are interconnected disciplines with some overlap.

Monetary Policy

Economics is a social science that studies the production, use, and distribution of products and services to better understand how economies function and how people interact. Modern economics is mostly very quantitative and highly math-oriented, despite being considered a "social science" and mostly regarded as one of the liberal arts. Macroeconomics and microeconomics are the two major divisions of economics.

Macroeconomics is a branch of economics that studies the behavior of the entire economy. Some economy-wide trends such as inflation, national income, gross domestic product (GDP), and increases in unemployment are extensively studied in macroeconomics.

Microeconomics is the analysis of economic tendencies, or what is likely to occur when people make certain decisions or when development factors alter. Microeconomics is concerned with the smaller factors that influence individual and corporate decisions, just as macroeconomics is concerned with how the economy as a whole behaves.

Microeconomics also outlines what to expect if such circumstances alter. Microeconomics predicts that if a car maker increases the price it sells its cars for, customers would purchase fewer cars than before. Since supply is limited, if a large copper mine in South America fails, copper prices are likely to rise.

Macroeconomics can be used to monitor GDP, inflation, and deficits to assist investors in making better decisions. Microeconomics may be able to explain why Apple Inc. stock prices may decline if customers purchase fewer iPhones. Microeconomics can also explain why a higher minimum wage can cause a business to recruit fewer employees.

Particular Points to Consider

When economists are effective in their goals of understanding how consumers and producers react to changing circumstances, economics can provide powerful guidance and impact to national policy-making. In other words, how governments handle taxation, policy, and government spending has real consequences; economics may provide insight and interpretation into these decisions.

Economic analysis may also assist investors in determining the impact of national policy and events on market conditions. Understanding economics will equip investors with the information they need to forecast macroeconomic conditions and assess the effects of such forecasts on businesses, stocks, and financial markets.

Academics is a choice for those interested in pursuing a career in economics. Academics invest their time not only teaching students economics concepts but also conducting research and developing new ideas and hypotheses for how markets operate and how their agents communicate.

Economists work in a variety of settings, including investment banks, consulting companies, and other businesses. Economists' responsibilities can include forecasting GDP, interest rates, inflation, and overall market conditions. Economists offer insight and forecasts that can help a business sell its product or serve as guidance for managers and other decision-makers.

Market investors may use economics to better understand the causes and possible consequences of market events, as well as the effect on different industries, businesses, and the overall business cycle.

Understanding how changes in national income, inflation, long-term economic growth, and interest rates affect the markets and, eventually, stocks, is one of the applications of economics. Economists are interested in deciding how shifts in monetary policy by central banks such as the Federal Reserve of the United States can affect the economy in the United States and around the world.

Chapter 2

PERSONAL FINANCES

Many people are shocked to discover that they spent more than they thought on their bank and credit card statements month after month. Personal financial statements are a straightforward way of accounting for income and expenses that can help you prevent this issue. Financial statements, like those used by companies, give you an idea of your financial situation and will help you prepare your budget. Personal financial statements are divided into two categories:

· A personal cash flow statement is a statement that shows how much money you have coming in

· The personal financial statement

Let's take a closer look at these.

Essential Takeaways

· You should make your financial statements to help you prepare your budget and set targets for growing your net worth.

·The personal cash flow statement and the personal balance sheet are the two forms of personal financial statements.

· The personal cash flow statement calculates whether you have a positive or negative net cash flow by comparing your cash inflows (money you earn) to your cash outflows (money you spend).

· To measure your net worth, a personal balance sheet summarizes your assets and liabilities.

Statement of Personal Cash Flow

A personal cash flow statement calculates your cash inflows and outflows to determine your net cash flow for a given period. The following are examples of cash inflows:

· Pay scales

· Savings accounts' interest

· Capital income from the sale of financial instruments such as stocks and bonds · Dividends from investments

Money earned from the sale of properties such as houses or cars may also be counted as cash inflow. Something that brings money into your business is considered cash inflow.

All expenses, regardless of amount, are represented by cash outflow. The following expenses are included in cash outflows:

· Payments for rent or mortgage

· Bills for utilities

· Groceries

· Gasoline

· Recreation (books, movie tickets, restaurant meals, etc.)

The aim of calculating cash inflows and outflows is to figure out your net cash flow. Simply subtracting your outflow from your inflow yields your net cash flow. A positive net cash flow indicates that you made more than you invested over time and that you have some money left over. A negative net cash balance, on the other hand, indicates that you expended more money than you took in.

Personal Financial Statement

The second form of the personal financial statement is a balance sheet. A personal balance sheet is a snapshot of the financial situation at a given point in time. It's a list of your assets (what you own), liabilities (what you owe), and net worth (how much money you have). Net worth is determined by subtracting your liabilities from your assets.

Possessions

Assets can be categorized into three categories:

· Liquid Assets (Liquid Assets): Liquid assets are items that can be quickly sold or converted to cash without losing value. Checking accounts, money market accounts, savings accounts, and cash are examples. Some people include certificates of deposit (CDs) in this category, but CDs have the disadvantage of charging an early withdrawal fee, which reduces the value of your investment.

· Large Assets: Homes, vehicles, vessels, artwork, and furniture are examples of large assets. Be sure to use the market value of these products when building a personal balance sheet. If determining a market value is difficult, compare recent sales prices of comparable goods.

Bonds, futures, CDs, mutual funds, and real estate are all examples of investments. You should also keep track of assets at their current market value.

Responsibilities

Liabilities are simply the debts that you owe. Present bills, interest already outstanding on some properties such as vehicles and homes, credit card balances, and other loans are all examples of liabilities.

Two common methods for paying off liabilities, such as credit card debt, are the "debt avalanche" and the "debt snowball."

Estimated Net Worth

The disparity between what you own and what you owe is your net worth. This is your wealth measurement because it reflects what you own after all of your debts have been paid off. If your net worth is negative, it means you owe more than you own.

Increasing your assets or decreasing your liabilities are two ways to boost your net worth. Assets can be increased by increasing cash or increasing the value of any asset you possess. However, I want to give you one word of warning: Make sure your liabilities don't develop in lockstep with your assets.

If you purchase a home, for example, your assets will increase, but if you take out a mortgage on it, your liabilities will increase as well. Increasing your net worth by increasing your assets would only work if your assets grow faster than your liabilities. Attempting to reduce liabilities is the same. A debt reduction must be greater than a reduction in assets.

Connecting the Dots

Personal financial statements provide you with the resources you need to keep track of your spending and develop your wealth. Personal financial statements are unique in that they are not simply two independent pieces of data, but rather operate in tandem. The cash flow statement's net cash flow will potentially assist you in your attempt to maximize your net worth. If your net cash flow is positive over a given time, you can use the money to buy assets or pay down debt. Applying your net cash flow to your net worth is a perfect way to grow your assets without raising your liabilities, or to reduce your liabilities without growing your assets.

Analyze the Outgoing

It's a good idea to review your finances regularly, particularly if you're planning a big purchase like a new car or home, or if your income or expenditures have changed significantly. Fortunately, you have access to the majority of the details you need. Take these measures when assessing your finances to ensure you're making informed choices that will help you plan for the future.

Make a Monthly Spending Plan

1. Add up your earnings. To make a monthly budget, start by listing all of your monthly income, including wages, interest, pensions, and any other sources of income, such as a spouse's income. If you are paid a wage, make sure to include your net pay rather than your gross pay. Remember to add taxes as a separate payment if they aren't deducted directly from your paycheck.
2. Make a budget for your expenditures. Keeping track of how much you spend in a month is the easiest way to do this. Check out the resources provided by your checking account, such as uploading credit or debit card statements or scanning receipts with your mobile, to keep track of your spending. Divide the expenses into fixed costs (those that don't vary from month to months, such as rent and insurance pay-

ments) and variable costs (those that change from month to month, such as food and entertainment). If any of your monthly expenditures vary greatly, measure the monthly cost using a three-month average of the total for that group.

3. Determine the distinction. Subtract the spending total from the revenue total to get the difference after you've totaled your yearly income and expenditures. It's a straightforward procedure that can show a great deal about your spending habits. Congratulations if the outcome is a good number; you are paying less than you make. If it's negative, your outgoings exceed your revenue, and you'll need to cut back on them and start living within your means.
4. Keep track of it. Monitor your monthly revenue and expenditures to ensure you stay on track with your spending plan. It may take some time to find the right balance for you.

Create a Rainy Day Fund

It's important to safeguard the money you've set aside for the future after you've created your budget. Do you have money set aside in case of an unexpected big expense? Building a large emergency fund that covers three to six months of living expenses is critical to establishing a solid financial base. Be sure to plan for emergency fund savings while reevaluating your finances so that you're prepared to manage any unexpected costs. Consider how you should set aside money per month to start building or growing an established savings account. To get started, use the Emergency Fund Calculator.

Organize The Debt Load

Take the time to decide how to most quickly pay off your debts, whether you're paying off a mortgage or student debt. Managing your debt burden — the balance of all of your debts — will assist you in improving your financial situation. Reducing these fees is a crucial step toward bettering the financial situation.

Analyze the Family

Budgeting has a bad rep among many Americans, who see it as a way to take all of the fun out of saving money. There will be no more shopping. There will be no more dining out in restaurants. Weekend golfing is no longer an option.

A budget is not intended to take parts of your lifestyle away.. It merely lays out how much money you have coming in and how you want to spend it. Since a budget lets you get the most out of your money, it's one of the most important tools in creating a prosperous financial future.

Any customer, regardless of their financial situation or generation, will profit from designing and managing a budget. A budget gives people a sense of financial stability. It can be thought of as a financial base. Each person's foundation will be unique, just as each person's financial situation will be unique.

Making a Financial Plan

Budgeting methods and tactics differ from one organization to the next. There would be distinctions between what works for a first-year college student and what works for a retiree, for example. However, there are five fundamental steps to making a budget. They're all vital because they build on one another, assisting you in effectively organizing your finances.

Step 1: Make a List of Your Objectives.

There are two types of financial objectives: short-term and long-term. Immediate goals are concerned with how you will invest your money now, while long-term goals are concerned with how you will save and spend your money for many years. Both are critical, and they work well together. Saving money now has an impact not just on what you spend now, but also on how much money you will have later in life.

You'll need to figure out which targets are for essentials and which are for extras. You will then prioritize your financial objectives accordingly.

Covering existing costs is one of the most pressing financial objectives. Your mortgage or rent payment, car loans, utility bills, child care, food, mobile phone, and household supplies are some of these that are needed. Non-essential clothes, subscriptions, eating out, and holidays are examples of secondary targets, also known as luxury products. Retirement savings, investments, and charitable contributions are also examples of long-term financial objectives. If you have debt, it is both necessary and optional to pay it off. Making needed payments is critical to financial stability, but paying off debt early, even if it is not required, will save money in the long run.

Step 2: Determine Your Earnings and Expenses

Once you've determined your financial objectives, you'll need to devise a strategy for achieving them. To do so, you must first assess your revenue and expenditures. Since most expenses are paid every month, most people budget monthly.

Make a list of all of your monthly income sources, including your salary (after taxes), any annual incentives, and child support or alimony payments. You can use an approximation if you don't know the exact number. Attach the numbers until you have them. Your monthly salary is the sum of all of your earnings.

Your expenditures, which are divided into fixed committed expenses, variable committed expenses, and discretionary expenses, are the next part of the equation.

Fixed committed expenses, such as your mortgage or rent, have a set monthly number.

Groceries and fuel are examples of variable committed expenses that vary from month to month depending on need.

Discretionary expenses are expenses that are not needed, such as leisure and entertainment. A gym membership will be included in this group as well. Discretionary expenses can make life more enjoyable, but if you can't afford the necessities, they should be the first to go.

If you don't pay off your credit card bills on time each month, you'll start paying a lot of interest. Any budget can be thrown into disarray as a result of this. You can see a nonprofit credit counselor if your carried-over credit card expenses consume more than 10% of your monthly revenue. A free credit counseling session can walk you through your budget over the phone or online and recommend expenditures that can be minimized or removed. You will be able to lower your monthly loan payments if you apply for a debt management program.

Step 3: Review Your Spending and Make a Checkbook Balance

Budgeting aims to ensure that your expenses do not surpass your revenue. If they do, and you're losing money faster than you're making money, you'll need to make some changes. This doesn't mean you should start pinching pennies; it simply means it's time to reconsider your discretionary spending to see if you're willing and able to trim the fat.

Your checkbook ledger will help you keep track of incoming and outgoing money, as well as what you spend it on if you make any payments by check. While paying by check is becoming less common, those who do so should keep their checkbooks in order. This will save you money on overdraft fees and bounced checks, as well as provide insight into your spending patterns.

Here are the fundamentals:

Keep track of all your transactions and deposits. Everyone should be documented in your checkbook, which you will receive from the bank.

If you don't already get one in the mail, print or download your monthly bank statement. If you're doing it online, there's software that can help you with this phase, as well as budgeting.

Create your calculations for deposits and withdrawals to ensure your bank hasn't overlooked anything or taken advantage of your funds. Reconcile line by line, ensuring that your check record matches the assertion.

Act backward from the ending number on each monthly statement, checking to see what has cleared and what has not. Deposits that haven't cleared must be deducted from your account balance. If your checks haven't cleared, they'll be deducted from your account before they do.

Account for any fees you're paying line by line. When you see them up close, you will decide to call and request that any be withdrawn, which the banks would usually do if you continue. Include any interest you might have got in your calculations.

This method can be automated using financial tools or applications if you have access to a computer or even a smartphone, saving you time and frustration. The aim is to go over your cash flow, look for mistakes, and learn from them.

Step 4: Go Through the Original Budget Again

After a month or two of tracking your income and expenditures, you'll be more conscious of areas that need to be changed. Perhaps your original monthly income figures were off, or you failed to budget for costs such as car repairs or veterinary bills. Make changes as required, but always keep inflows and outflows in balance.

Once you've ironed out all the kinks in your budget, you must commit to sticking to it. However, since no budget lasts forever, it's important to revisit it regularly.

You will increase your discretionary expenses as well as your savings targets if you get a promotion, for example. A layoff or reduced work hours, on the other hand, can necessitate spending cuts before your income is restored.

Savings should be a part of your strategy. Financial planners suggest that you save six months' worth of income to cover a work loss or other unexpected event. Opening a separate savings account and progressively funding it before you meet your target can be beneficial. It would be more difficult to use the emergency fund to cover non-essential expenses if you keep a separate account.

Step 5: Commitment

Making a budget is an excellent first step toward ensuring a more financially secure future for you and your family. You'll get there if you stick to your budget. Keep it practical, check it often, and don't be afraid to make changes. It's all about striking a balance when it comes to budgeting.

How to Manage Your Budget When Unexpected Bills ArriveAn emergency fund, as previously said, is critical to financial stability. Start by setting aside $50 per week. That would give you $2,600 in a year, plus any interest, for when the refrigerator breaks down or the transmission fails.

To find hidden cash, experts recommend looking at your withholding taxes. If you get a big refund every year, you may want to consider changing your filing status to get more money in your paycheck to put into an emergency fund (unless you're putting money from your tax refund into that fund).

Medical emergencies, in particular, can throw a budget into disarray. Negotiate major care bills with the hospital, such as an emergency hospital stay. Almost every hospital agrees to a fee arrangement. The hospital or provider's office will also set up a payment schedule if you contact them right away rather than waiting until the bill is sent to collections.

If not, a medical bill consolidation service or a bank loan might be able to help you consolidate all of your medical bills into one lower monthly bill. This plan not only makes it simpler for you, but also preserves your credit score by allowing you to make on-time payments. The disadvantage is that it will take you longer to pay off your debt completely.

Chapter 3

PLANNING A PERSONAL BUDGET

You'll need a budget if you want to keep track of your finances and achieve your financial goals.

A personal or household budget is a list of your income and expenditures for a certain period, usually one month. Although the word "budget" conjures up images of restricted spending, a budget doesn't need to trim spending to be successful.

A budget will show you how much money you plan to bring in, as well as your required expenditures (like rent and insurance) and discretionary spending (like entertainment or dining out). Rather than seeing a budget as a hindrance, think of it as a vehicle for achieving your financial objectives.

What Does a Budget Do?

A monthly budget is a written financial planning tool that helps you to schedule how much money you'll spend or save each month. You should also keep track of your spending habits.

Making a budget does not sound like the most enjoyable thing (though it is for some), but it is an essential part of keeping your financial house in order. Spending less in one sector allows you to spend more in another, save for a big purchase, create a "rainy day" fund, raise your savings, or invest in wealth building.

A budget can only succeed if you are completely realistic about your income and expenditures. You must be able to work with comprehensive and reliable details about your earning and spending patterns to create an efficient budget.

Finally, the outcome of your new budget will reveal where your money comes from, how much you have, and where it all goes each month.

How to Build a Budget in Six Easy Steps

Find a suitable template to fill in the numbers for your expenditures and revenue before you start making a budget.

Although you can budget your money with pen and paper, using a monthly budget spreadsheet or a budgeting app is simpler and more effective. These will have allocated fields for different categories of income and expenditures, as well as built-in formulas to help you find out your budget surplus or deficit with minimal effort.

1. Gather all of your financial documents

   Gather all of your financial statements before you begin, including:

   · W-2s and paystubs

   · 1099s

- Bank statements
- Investment reports
- Recent energy bills
- Bills from credit cards
- Last three months' receipts
- Mortgage or car loan statements

You want to be able to see all of your revenue and spending records. Creating a monthly average is one of the most important aspects of the budgeting process. The more data you can gather, the better.

2. Determine Your Earnings

What kind of monthly income can you expect? Using the net salary (or take-home pay) figure is fine if the income is in the form of a daily paycheck with taxes deducted automatically. Include any outside sources of income, such as child care or Social Security, if you are self-employed. Make a monthly total of your total revenue. Consider using the salary from your lowest-earning month in the previous year as your average income when creating your budget if you have a variable income (for example, from a seasonal or freelance job).

3. Make a monthly expense list.

Make a list of all the expenses you intend to incur over a month. This list may include things like

- Mortgage or rent payments
- Vehicle payments
- Insurance
- Groceries
- Utilities
- Entertainment
- Personal care
- Eating out

- Childcare
- Transportation expenses
- Travel
- Student loans
- Savings

To monitor your expenses, go through your bank statements, receipts, and credit card statements from the previous three months.

4. Calculate Fixed and Variable Costs

Fixed expenses are those that must be paid regularly and for which you pay the same amount each time. Include fees for a mortgage or rent, a car, a fixed-fee internet service, garbage collection, and routine childcare. Include any other important spending that appears to remain the same from month to month if you pay a regular credit card bill.

Include savings and debt reduction as fixed expenses if you intend to save a certain sum or pay off a set amount of debt each month.

Groceries, gasoline, entertainment, eating out, and gifts are examples of variable expenditures that vary from month to month.

If you don't have an emergency fund, set aside money for "surprise expenditures" that can arise during the month and throw your budget off track.

Beginning with your fixed expenditures, assign a spending value to each group. Then figure out how much you'll need to spend on variable expenses per month.

If you're not sure how much you pay in each group, look over your credit card or bank statements from the past two or three months to get an idea.

5. Add up your monthly earnings and expenses.
   You're on the right track if your revenue exceeds your expenditures. This extra cash allows you to allocate funds to other parts of your budget, such as retirement savings or debt repayment.
   Start using the "50-30-20" budgeting philosophy if your revenue exceeds your expenditures. In a 50-30-20 budget, "needs," or necessary expenditures, should account for half of your budget, "wants" should account for another 30%, and savings and debt repayment should account for the remaining 20%.
   If your expenditures exceed your revenue, you're overspending and need to make some adjustments.
6. Make Expense Adjustments

Find places in your variable spending to cut if your expenses are higher than your revenue. Look for ways to save costs, such as dining out less, or delete a category, such as canceling your gym membership.

If your expenses exceed your income or you have a lot of debt, lowering your variable expenses may not be enough. To balance your budget, you will need to lower your fixed expenses and raise your revenue.

Aim for a balance in the revenue and cost tables. This fair balance indicates that all of your earnings have been paid for and allocated to a particular cost or investment target.

How to Make the Most of Your Budget

You must control and continue to track your expenditures in each category after you have set up your budget, preferably every day of the month. The same spreadsheet or software that you used to create your budget can also be used to keep track of your expenses and revenue.

Keeping track of your expenditures during the month can help you avoid overspending and recognize excessive or problematic spending trends. Rather than waiting for the end of the month to report your expenses, take a few minutes per day to do so.

If you're not sure you can budget your money, use the envelope scheme, which divides the cash into separate envelopes for various categories of spending. When an envelope is empty, you must avoid spending in that category.

Keep track of how much you've spent when you go through your budget. You'll need to either stop spending in that category for the month or transfer money from another category to cover extra expenditures once you've hit your spending cap in that category.

Your budget's target should be to keep your monthly expenditures equal to or less than your monthly revenue.

Budgeting Advice

Once you've created a simple budget, you can tailor it to your specific financial condition and goals.

1. If you work on commission, save aggressively to help cover downturns in the economy.
2. If you're having cash flow problems and you're only paying once a month, split your payment into weeks and put the money you planned to spend in the remaining weeks in a different account before you need it.
3. Only use a credit card if you know you'll be able to pay it off at the end of the month. Otherwise, you'll be charged interest on top of the purchase price.

4. If you notice that you have overestimated or underestimated your expenditures, make monthly adjustments to your budget. Keep track of major costs that arise only once or twice a year, such as insurance premiums.
5. Using budgeting hacks like going to a cash-only budget if you plan to overspend on those categories.
6. Once your expenditures are less than your income, set aside money for investments before increasing your spending.
7. Make time to develop your financial literacy and make your money work harder for you by learning other financial skills.

12 Steps to Making a Budget – Personal Budgeting Advice for Newbies

Creating the first budget can be a daunting task. How overwhelming is it that only 40% of American families have a monthly budget that they can stick to. However, the effort is well worth it. Creating a budget that you can stick to over time has been shown to help you create wealth while also assisting you in getting out of debt and reducing expenses.

If you're a first-time budgeter, follow these 12 simple steps to make the process go as smoothly as possible.

1. Decide to begin a budget.
   If you're reading this, you've probably already decided to start a working budget. Congratulations on your achievement! This is the most difficult thing for many people, including myself. Continue reading to learn about the next steps.

2. Be aware of your financial situation.
   If you have savings, checking, investment, or other financial accounts, you'll need to know how much money is in each, as well as the interest rates and fees associated with each. Make a mental note of this data. It will play a role in deciding your net worth and the best way to invest your money in the future.
   If you use Personal Capital to create your budget, this information will be pulled in automatically.
3. Figure Out Your Earnings
   Some people find it simpler than others to determine their earnings. Those on a salaried salary will accurately calculate their monthly earnings. It can be much more complicated for hourly workers or those who work in a sector where compensation fluctuates wildly. The most important consideration, regardless of how you make your monthly profits, is to figure out how much money you make every month.
   If you have intermittent income, averaging the last 6 to 12 months of recurring income and using that number is a safe way to go. If you want to be extra cautious, choose the lowest monthly number you paid in the previous year, which should give you a good idea of the worst-case scenario.
4. Recognize What You Owe
   The next move should be to determine your monthly recurring debt payments. As long as you haven't taken on any new debt in the short term, this should be relatively easy. It's fine if you haven't been able to shake your credit card addiction. Making a budget is the first step toward achieving the next financial goal: paying off high-interest consumer debt.

Calculate the cumulative amount due on each debt account as well as the minimum monthly payment to determine the monthly recurring debt payments. This includes car loans, mortgages, credit card debt, student loans, and any other debt the family is responsible for every month.

This will give you the first few line items in your budget and help you to figure out how much money you have.

If you're still paying off student loans, refinancing with Credible might be able to lower your interest rate. They're now offering a $750 incentive if you refinance your student loans.

5. Work Out Your Net Worth

You can quickly measure your net worth once you know how much money you have and how much you owe. Simply deduct the amount you owe from the amount you have. The response will reveal the worth of your financial assets.

This number was a real eye-opener for me. I had a negative net worth when I produced my first budget. I think this is fairly common in America, especially among young people who are just starting to manage their finances.

When you sign up for Personal Capital, you will add all of your financial accounts and your net worth will be calculated automatically.

6. Calculate Your Average Monthly Recurring Expenses

This is a difficult task for many individuals. Making a one-month stack of household expenses is the easiest way to figure out your monthly expenses. Keep track of your receipts, gas bills, and any other expenses that occur over a month, then sort them into categories. You may make the categories as wide or as narrow as you like. I keep my categories wide (automotive/household), while you might prefer itemized categories like car wash/electric bill. It doesn't matter which way you go as long as you figure out an average amount of expenses for each category.

7. Make a Database With This Information

   Budgets used to be made up of old-fashioned paper ledgers. For modern budgeters, things have changed for the better. Microsoft Excel and online budgeting resources such as Personal Capital, Mint, You Need a Budget, and Mvelopes make creating a highly adjustable and manageable long-term budget a lot simpler.

   For my budget, I use Microsoft Excel because it gives me more versatility than places like Mint. Many people, on the other hand, swear by online budgeting pages. Whichever direction you take will help you accumulate more money and stay out of debt in the long run.

   Pro tip: Tiller is a good option if you want the ease of an online budgeting tool but prefer the functionality of an Excel document. Tiller syncs your everyday transactions to a Google Sheet or Excel spreadsheet.

8. Pay Attention to the Bottom Line

   You'll find the most important number in your budgeting phase after entering all of the above data: the bottom line. This figure will indicate whether you are overspending or underspending.

   Ideally, you'll discover that you're living within your means – and that you have some money left over each month. On the other hand, you might find that you need to change your monthly expenditures to stay within your budget.

9. Make Alterations as a Result
   If your budget's bottom line reveals that you're over-spending, the next move is the most difficult: reducing your monthly expenses. Money Crashers has a lot of tools to help you be smarter with your money, cut your recurring monthly expenditures, and stay on track with your budget in the future.
10. Make any Necessary Adjustments
    Life is full of unexpected twists and turns. Food prices go up, gas prices go up, and rent goes up when you least expect it. You must change your expense categories based on your current reality if you note inflation creeping up on your expense categories, receive a raise at work, or experience a financial setback such as a pay cut or job loss.
11. Take Care of Yourself First
    You may want to add a few extra line items to your monthly expenditures based on your bottom line. This may be monthly deposits into a CIT Bank, Capital One 360, or Ally Bank savings account; a Roth IRA; a 529 college savings plan; or another savings vehicle. Moving money into savings and treating it as a recurring cost helps you to gradually build up your savings without feeling obligated to pick together money from the end of the month's leftovers.

    A Chime bank account is another choice for saving. Chime automates the deposit of 10% of each paycheck into your savings account, allowing you to pay yourself first.

12. Keep Track of What You're Doing and How You're Doing it

It takes about an hour a week to keep track of your budget. However, it will save you a significant amount of time in the long run. If you've formed a budget, make sure to stick to it. Knowing you're making sound long- and short-term financial decisions will give you a lot of peace of mind. It will also help you transition from living paycheck to paycheck to being able to see the fruits of your careful saving and budgeting.

Final Thoughts

Now is the time to make a budget if you don't already have one. You'll be on the way to financial independence and future prosperity if you take the steps above.

Do you have a well-thought-out personal budget? What has succeeded and what hasn't for you?

Chapter 4

INCOME AND CASH FLOW STATEMENT

What is the difference between a profit and loss statement and a balance sheet?

The income statement is one of three main financial statements used to report a company's financial results for a particular accounting period, with the balance sheet and the statement of cash flows being the other two.

The income statement, also known as the profit and loss statement or the statement of revenue and cost, reports on the company's sales and expenditures for a specific period.

Essential Takeaways

· An income statement is one of the three main financial statements that records a company's financial results for a particular accounting period (along with the balance sheet and the statement of cash flows).

· Net income is calculated as follows: (Total Revenue + Gains) – (Total Expenses + Losses).

· Total income is the amount of operating and non-operating profits, while total expenditures are the sum of primary and secondary activities' expenses.

· Revenues are not the same as receipts. On the income statement, revenue is received and published. Receipts (cash collected or paid out) are not considered receipts.

· An income statement will reveal a lot about a company's activities, management effectiveness, underperforming markets, and results in comparison to industry peers.

An income statement is a financial statement that indicates how profitable the company was during a particular reporting period. It displays your income after subtracting your expenditures and losses.

The income statement, along with the balance sheet and the cash flow statement, is one of the three most relevant financial statements in financial accounting. It is also known as a "net income statement" or a "statement of earnings" (or statement of cash flows).

When a bank or investor needs to see how profitable a company is, small businesses usually start generating income statements.

When a company prepares an income statement solely for internal use, it's often referred to as a "profit and loss statement" (or P&L).

Revenue, expenses, gains, and losses are the four main items on the income statement. It makes no distinction between cash and non-cash receipts (cash transactions vs. credit sales) or cash vs. non-cash payments/disbursements (purchases in cash versus purchases on credit). It begins with sales data, then works its way down to calculate net income and, finally, earnings per share (EPS). It essentially explains how the company's net income is converted into net earnings (profit or loss).

Gains and Revenues

The income statement includes the following items, though the format may differ based on local regulatory requirements, the business's diversified scope, and the related operating activities:

Revenue from Operations

Operating revenue is a term used to describe revenue generated by primary operations. The revenue from primary activities refers to revenue generated from the sale of a commodity by a company that manufactures it, or by a wholesaler, distributor, or retailer who is in the business of selling it. Similarly, income from primary operations refers to the revenue or fees received in return for providing such services by a corporation (or its franchisees) in the service sector.

Revenue from Non-Operating Activities

Non-operating recurring revenues are revenues generated from non-core business operations that are not part of the core business. These profits come from sources other than the purchase and sale of goods and services, such as interest gained on business capital in the bank, rental income from business property, income from strategic relationships such as royalty payment receipts, or income from an advertising show on business property.

Benefits

Gains, also known as other profits, are the net proceeds from other investments such as the sale of long-term properties. Net income from one-time non-business operations, such as a company selling an old transportation van, unused property, or a subsidiary company, is included in this category.

The terms "revenue" and "receipts" are not interchangeable. The time in which purchases are made or services are rendered is typically when revenue is recorded. Receipts are the receipts of cash that are recorded when the money is paid. For example, a customer may purchase products or services from a company on September 28, resulting in revenue being recorded in September. The customer could be granted a 30-day payment window due to his good reputation. That would give them until the 28th of October to make the payment when the receipts will be accounted for.

Losses and Expenses

A loss is the cost of a company continuing to operate and making a profit. If you follow the IRS requirements, you will be able to deduct any of these costs on your tax return.

Expenses for the Main Activity

These costs are incurred to generate regular operating income from the business's primary operation. Cost of goods sold (COGS); selling, general, and administrative expenses (SG&A); depreciation or amortization; and research and development (R&D) expenses are all examples of these expenses. Employee salaries, sales fees, and expenditures for services like energy and transportation are common things on the list.

Expenses for Extracurricular Activities

These costs are related to non-core company operations, such as interest on borrowed funds.

Expenses as Losses

There are any costs associated with a loss-making sale of long-term assets, one-time or other unexpected costs, or litigation costs.

Although primary revenue and expenses provide information about the company's core business, secondary revenue and expenses reflect the company's involvement and experience in managing ad-hoc, non-core activities. A significantly high interest income from money in the bank, as compared to income from the sale of manufactured goods, means that the company is either not using the available cash to its maximum potential by expanding manufacturing capacity, or it is having difficulty raising its market share due to competition. The business factory's recurring rental income from hosting billboards along a highway means that the management is maximizing the available resources and assets for increased profitability.

Structure of the Income Statement

The following is how the Net Income is measured mathematically:

(Revenue + Gains) – (Expenses + Losses) = Net Income

Income Statements Have a Wide Range of Applications

Though the primary aim of an income statement is to inform stakeholders about the company's performance and financial practices, it also offers quantitative insights into the company's internals for comparison across various companies and industries. Such statements are often prepared more regularly at the department and division levels for company management to obtain deeper perspectives and check the progress of different operations during the year, though such interim reports remain internal to the company.

Management may make decisions based on income statements such as expanding into new geographies, moving revenue, growing manufacturing capability, increasing asset usage or outright selling, or shutting down a department or product line. Competitors can also use them to learn about a company's performance metrics and focus areas, such as can R&D spending.

Creditors may find income statements to be of limited use because they are more concerned with a company's potential cash flows than its past profitability. The income statement is used by research analysts to assess year-over-year and quarter-over-quarter results. One can conclude whether a company's efforts to lower the cost of sales helped it boost income over time, or whether management was able to keep operating expenses under control without sacrificing profitability.

The Selling Price of Products

This is how much it costs you to manufacture all of the goods or services you sold to your clients. This figure is abbreviated as "COGS."

COGS consists solely of direct costs such as raw materials, labor, and shipping. This may include the expense of raw coffee beans, salaries, and packaging if you roast and sell coffee like Coffee Roaster Enterprises.

Indirect costs such as electricity, bank fees, and rent are not included in COGS and are tracked separately.

Benefit Before Taxes

Deducting total COGS from sales will give you the benefit before taxes. Gross profit indicates how profitable the company is after direct expenses have been deducted but before overhead costs have been deducted. It's a rough estimate of your company's performance.

Expenses in General

Rent, bank & ATM fee expenses, equipment expenses, marketing & advertisement expenses, merchant fees, and any other expenses you need to make to keep your company running are all examples of operating expenses.

These costs are reported separately here, but some income statements will group these and other related costs into a single category called "Selling, General, and Administrative Expenses" (SG&A).

Profits from Operations

This is the profit margin of your company after paying all its internal expenses that you have more control over, but paying its external costs, such as loan interest payments and taxes, that you have less control over.

This is often referred to as Operating Profit or Operating Income by accountants.

Expense for Interest

If your company owes someone money, it will almost certainly have to pay interest every month. The net interest payments the company made to its creditors for the period covered by the income statement are your interest expenses.

Earnings Before the Imposition of Income Taxes

This is the net margin of the company before taxes.

The Expense for Income Taxes

This is the sum you handed over to Uncle Sam.

Benefit After Taxes

Have you ever wondered where the phrase "bottom line" comes from? This is it! This figure is the company's net benefit at the end of the day.

Model for a Financial Statement

To make an income statement, you don't need expensive accounting software or a degree in accounting. Expert bookkeepers at Bench have created an Income Statement template in Excel that you can use to create an Income Statement from your company's financial data.

What is the Concept of a Single-step Income Statement?

Since you must conduct several calculations to arrive at your final net income, the income statement we gave you above is technically referred to as a "multi-step" income statement. In this case, we measured gross profit before deducting general expenditures, debt, and income tax expenses.

A single-step income statement is easier to understand. It calculates your net income by adding your total revenue and subtracting your total expenses. It's that simple.

Statement of Cash Flows

The cash flow statement, also known as the statement of cash flow, is a financial statement that summarizes the amount of cash and cash equivalents that enter and leave a company.

The cash flow statement (CFS) is a financial statement that shows how well a business handles its cash position, or how well it produces cash to cover debts and finance operating expenses. Since 1987, the cash flow statement has been a required component of a company's financial reporting in addition to the balance sheet and income statement.

Essential Takeaways

· A cash flow statement is a financial statement that shows how much cash and cash equivalents are coming in and going out of a company.

· A company's cash flow statement shows how well it handles its cash position, or how well it produces cash to meet debt commitments and cover operating expenses.

· Since 1987, the cash flow statement has been a required component of a company's financial reporting, complementing the balance sheet and income statement.

· Cash from operating operations, cash from investing activities, and cash from funding activities are the three primary components of the cash flow statement.

· The direct approach and the indirect method are the two approaches for measuring cash flow.

What Is a Cash Flow Statement and How Can I Use It?

Investors may use the CFS to understand how a company's operations work, where its money comes from, and how it is spent. The CFS is important because it aids investors in determining whether a business is financially sound.

Creditors, on the other hand, may use the CFS to figure out how much cash is available (also known as liquidity) for the business to cover operating costs and pay its debts.

The Cash Flow Statement's Structure

The following are the key components of the cash flow statement:

1. Income from business operations
2. Income from investment activities
3. Funding activities generate cash
4. Non-cash transactions are often disclosed when financial statements are compiled following commonly accepted accounting standards (GAAP).

Since it does not contain the amount of potential incoming and outgoing cash that has been reported on credit, the CFS is distinct from the income statement and balance sheet. As a result, cash is not the same as net profits, which covers all cash and credit sales on the income statement and balance sheet.

Cash Generated From Operations

Any sources and uses of cash from company operations are included in the operational activities on the CFS. In other words, it shows how much money a business makes from its goods or services.

Cash from operations generally reflects cash adjustments, accounts receivable, depreciation, inventory, and accounts payable.

The following are examples of operational activities:

- Receipts for goods and services sold
- Payments of interest
- Payments in income taxes
- Payments to manufacturers of products and services used in the manufacturing process
- Paying workers' salaries and wages
- Fees for rent
- All other kinds of running costs

Receipts from the sale of loans, debt, or equity instruments are often included in the case of a trading fund or an investment firm. Depreciation, amortization, deferred tax, profits or losses associated with a noncurrent asset, and dividends or revenue earned from such investment activities are also included when preparing a cash flow statement using the indirect process. Long-term asset acquisitions and sales, on the other hand, are not included in operational activities.

How to Calculate Cash Flow

Cash flow is measured by adding or subtracting changes in sales, expenditures, and credit transactions (appearing on the balance sheet and income statement) arising from transactions that occur from one time to the next from net income. Non-cash items are factored into net income (income statement) and total assets and liabilities, so these changes are essential (balance sheet). As a result, certain items must be re-evaluated when measuring cash flow from operations since not all transactions contain real cash items.

As a consequence, there are two different approaches for estimating cash flow: direct and indirect.

Method of Direct Cash Flow

The direct system totals all cash payments and receipts, including cash charged to vendors, cash received from consumers, and cash paid out in wages. These statistics are derived by comparing the beginning and ending balances of several different business accounts and calculating the net decrease or rise in the accounts.

Method of Indirect Cash Flow

The indirect approach calculates cash flow from operating activities by subtracting net profits from a company's income statement first. Revenue is only remembered when it is paid, not when it is collected, since a company's income statement is prepared on an accrual basis. Since net income does not accurately reflect net cash flow from operating operations, earnings before interest and taxes (EBIT) must be adjusted for things that impair net income, even though no real cash has been collected or spent against them. Non-operating operations that do not impact a company's operating cash flow are often added back using the indirect form.

Depreciation, for example, is a sum removed from the net value of an asset that has already been paid for; it is not a cash cost. That is why it is added back into net sales when measuring cash flow.

The only time an asset's income is factored into CFS equations is when it is sold.

Cash Flow and Accounts Receivable

Cash flow must represent changes in accounts receivable (AR) on the balance sheet from one accounting period to the next. If accounts receivable falls, it means that more money has reached the business as a result of consumers paying off their credit cards; the difference in AR and net revenue is then added together. Since the sums expressed in AR are income but not currency, whether they increase from one accounting period to the next, the value of the increase must be deducted from net sales.

Cash Flow and Inventory Value

A rise in inventory, on the other hand, indicates that a business has spent more money on raw materials. The rise in the value of inventory is deducted from net sales if the inventory was paid in cash. Net revenues will be boosted by a reduction in inventory. If inventory was bought on credit, the balance sheet would show an increase in accounts payable, and the value of the increase from one year to the next would be applied to net sales.

Taxes due, wages due, and prepaid premiums all follow the same logic. When something has been paid off, net profits must be reduced by the difference in the amount due from one year to the next. Any disparities would have to be applied to net earnings if there is already a balance due.

Money Earned By Investing

Any sources and uses of cash from a company's assets are used in investing activities. This category includes the purchase or sale of an asset, loans made to suppliers or obtained from buyers, and any payments related to a merger or acquisition. In a nutshell, improvements in facilities, properties, or investments are related to the cash generated by investing.

Since cash is used to purchase new machinery, properties, or short-term assets such as marketable securities, cash changes from investing are usually a "cash-out" item. When a corporation sells an asset, however, the sale is counted as "cash in" when measuring cash flow from investments.

Financing Activities Result in Cash

The sources of cash from investors or banks, as well as the uses of cash charged to shareholders, are all included in cash from funding activities. Dividends, stock repurchase fees, and debt principal repayment (loans) are also included in this group.

When money is collected, changes in cash are "cash in," and when dividends are paid they are "cash out." When a company issues a bond to the public, it receives cash financing; when the company pays interest to bondholders, it reduces its cash.

The Statement of Cash Flows (also known as the cash flow statement) is one of three central financial statements that show how much money was made and spent over some time (e.g., a month, quarter, or year). By showing how money moved in and out of the company, the statement of cash flows serves as a link between the income statement and the balance sheet.

The Statement of Cash Flows is divided into three sections:

1. Operating Activities: An organization's primary revenue-generating activities as well as any non-investment or funding activities; any cash flows from existing assets and current liabilities.
2. Any cash flows from the purchase and sale of long-term assets and other transactions that are not included in cash equivalents are referred to as investing activities.
3. Any cash flows that result in changes in the size and composition of the entity's contributed equity capital or borrowings are referred to as financing activities (i.e., bonds, stock, dividends)

Classifications of Cash Flows

1. Cash Flow from Operations

   The entity's primary revenue-generating operations are its operating activities. The cash flows associated with sales, acquisitions, and other costs are usually included in cash flow from operations.

   The company's chief financial officer (CFO) decides whether to present operating cash flow directly or indirectly:

   · Direct Presentation: Operating cash flows are viewed as a list of cash flows, such as sales revenue, capital spending revenue, and so on. Since indirect presentation is more popular, this is a simple but rarely used form.

   · Indirect Presentation: Operating cash flows are

viewed as a profit-to-cash-flow reconciliation.

The cash flow statement does not include all real cash flows, but only "reasons why cash flow differs from profit."

Depreciation lowers earnings but has little effect on cash flow (it is a non-cash expense). As a result, it has been reinstated. Similarly, if the starting point benefit in the income statement is greater than interest and tax, interest and tax cash flows must be discounted before being counted as operating cash flows.

There is no clear recommendation for which benefit sum to use in the reconciliation. Operating profit, profit before tax, profit after tax, and net profits are all terms used by different businesses. The precise starting point for the reconciliation will dictate the exact changes that must be made to arrive at an operating cash flow figure.

2. Cash Flow Investing

   The purchase and sale of noncurrent assets and other investments not contained in cash equivalents are included in cash flow from investing activities. The cash flows associated with purchasing or selling land, plant, and equipment (PP&E); other noncurrent assets; and other financial assets are commonly referred to as investing cash flows.

   Capital expenditures (CapEx) are funds spent on buying PP&E.

3. Cash Flow Financing

Financing activities result in improvements in the size and composition of the entity's equity capital or borrowings, which are referred to as cash flow from financing activities. Borrowing and repaying bank loans, as well as selling and buying back securities, are both examples of financing cash flows. A dividend payment is often considered a financing cash flow.

Cash Flow and Interest

There are two ways to present interest costs in the cash flow statement under IFRS. Many businesses report operating cash flows that include both interest earned and interest charged. Others consider interest earned as an investment and interest charged as a financing cash flow. The process is determined by the finance director's preference.

Interest paid and collected are often considered as operating cash flows under U.S. GAAP.

Flow of Cash

Similar cash flow metrics are used by investment bankers and finance practitioners for different purposes. A common calculation used for DCF valuation is free cash flow. Free cash flow, on the other hand, has no clear meaning and can be measured and used in a variety of ways.

You will learn more in CFI's Ultimate Cash Flow Guide.

How Do I Make a Cash Flow Statement?

The direct method or the indirect method may be used to display the operating portion of the statement of cash flows. The investing and funding sections are the same in both methods; the only difference is in the operating section. The direct approach displays the most common types of gross cash receipts and payments. The indirect process, on the other hand, begins with net income and adjusts profit/loss for transaction results. In the end, whether using the direct or indirect method, cash flows from the operating segment will produce the same result; however, the presentation will differ.

The International Accounting Standards Board (IASB) prefers the direct method of reporting over the indirect method because it offers more useful information. However, it is estimated that more than 90% of businesses use the indirect approach.

Presentation Methods: Direct vs. Indirect

The direct method and the indirect method are the two ways to create a statement of cash flows.

In the direct process, all individual instances of cash collected or paid out are totaled, and the resultant cash flow is the sum.

To calculate cash flow using the indirect form, accounting line items such as net profits, depreciation, and so on are used. The indirect approach is used to create the cash flow statement in financial modeling.

What Does the Cash Flow Statement Tell Us?

· The quality of earnings can be determined by comparing cash from operating activities to net income. Earnings are said to be of "high quality" if cash from operating activities exceeds net income.

· This assertion is useful to investors since it helps them to get a general sense of the company's cash inflows and outflows, as well as a general understanding of its overall results since cash is king.

· If a business is covering operations losses or acquisitions by raising capital (debt or equity), it will show up on the statement of cash flows immediately.

Chapter 5

UNDERSTANDING ASSETS

A resource with economic value that a person, company, or country owns or controls with the expectation of future profit is referred to as an asset. Assets are purchased or produced to increase a company's wealth or support its operations, and they are listed on the balance sheet. Whether it's production equipment or a patent, an asset can be thought of as something that can produce cash flow, minimize costs, or increase revenue in the future.

Essential Takeaways

· An asset is a valuable resource that a person, company, or country owns or controls with the expectation of future profit.

· Assets are purchased or generated to increase a company's value or support its operations and are listed on the balance sheet.

· Whether it's production equipment or a patent, an asset can be thought of as something that can create cash flow, minimize costs, or increase revenue in the future.

Assets: An Overview

An asset is a financial advantage or access possessed by an organization that other people or businesses do not have. A legal right or other access means that economic resources can be used at the discretion of a corporation, and its use can be prohibited or restricted by the owner.

A business must have a claim to an asset as of the date of the financial statements for it to be present. An economic resource is something that is limited in supply and has the potential to generate an economic gain by increasing or decreasing cash inflows or outflows.

Short-term (or current) assets, fixed assets, capital instruments, and intangible assets are all types of assets.

Assets of Different Types

Assets in Use

Short-term economic resources that are supposed to be turned into cash within a year are referred to as current assets. Cash and cash equivalents, accounts receivable, inventory, and various prepaid expenditures are all examples of current assets.

Although cash is simple to value, accountants must reevaluate the recoverability of inventory and accounts receivable regularly. It may become affected if there is proof that accounts receivable could be uncollectible. Companies can also write off inventory if it becomes obsolete.

Assets are reported on balance sheets using the historical cost concept, which reflects the asset's original cost, adjusted for any changes or aging.

Fixed Assets

These are assets that cannot be changed. Plant, vehicles, and structures are examples of long-term capital. Depreciation is a periodic fee that may or may not represent the loss of earning power for a fixed asset. It is used to compensate for the aging of fixed assets.

Depreciation can be done in two ways, according to generally accepted accounting standards (GAAP). The straight-line approach assumes that the value of a fixed asset depreciates in proportion to its useful life, while the accelerated method assumes that the asset depreciates more rapidly in the first years of use.

Financial Resources

Financial assets are investments in other institutions' assets and shares. Stocks, sovereign and corporate bonds, preferred equity, and other hybrid instruments are examples of financial assets. The value of financial assets is determined by how the investment is classified and the motivation behind it.

Intangible Assets

Intangible assets are financial resources that do not have a physical location. Patents, trademarks, copyrights, and goodwill are among them. Intangible assets are treated differently based on their form, and they may be amortized or checked for damage each year.

A skilled appraiser is typically required to determine the worth of properties other than cash and cash equivalents. The cost method and the market value method are the two most popular methods for calculating asset value.

Since it uses the asset's original selling price, the cost approach is a straightforward way to value it. However, since the market value, or mark to market process, will decrease or increase from the initial purchasing price over time, it can be a more precise way of measuring asset value. The value of an asset is determined using this formula, which is based on the price at which it will sell on the open market.

Personal Property

Personal assets are items that a person or family owns that have current or potential value. Personal assets include the following items:

· Money and cash equivalents, certificates of deposit, checking and savings accounts, money market accounts, physical cash, and Treasury bills are all examples of financial instruments.

· Real estate or property, as well as any structures permanently affixed to it

· Personal property – vessels, collectibles, furniture, jewelry, and automobiles

· Annuities, shares, the cash value of life insurance programs, mutual funds, pensions, retirement savings (IRAs, 401(k), 403(b), and so on) securities

Subtracting your liabilities from your assets yields your net worth. Your assets are everything you own, while your liabilities are everything you owe. Positive net worth means your assets are worth more than your liabilities, while a negative net worth means your liabilities are worth more than your assets (in other words, you are in debt).

Assets in the Company

Assets are valuable items that help businesses continue to produce and expand. Machines, property, raw materials, and inventory - as well as intangibles like patents, royalties, and other intellectual property - are examples of assets for a company.

The balance sheet displays a company's assets as well as how those assets are funded, whether by debt or equity. The balance sheet shows how effectively a company's management is allocating its money. On a standard balance sheet, there are two types of properties.

Assets in Use

Current assets are assets that can be turned into cash in less than a fiscal year or operating period. Current assets are used to make day-to-day operations and acquisitions easier.

Present assets include the following:

· Cash and cash equivalents: Treasury bills, certificates of deposit, and currency are all examples of cash and cash equivalents.

· Debt or liquid securities, also known as marketable securities

· Accounts receivables: money owed by consumers that must be paid within a limited period.

· Inventory: ready-to-sell products or raw materials

Fixed Assets are assets that cannot be changed.

Noncurrent assets are assets that a business uses in the manufacture of products and services and have a life of more than one year. Fixed assets are listed as land, plant, and equipment on the balance sheet (PP&E). Fixed assets are long-term investments that are also known as tangible assets because they can be reached.

Fixed assets include the following:

· Automobiles (such as company trucks)

· Office equipment

· Equipment

· Structures

· Property

Noncurrent assets (such as fixed assets) cannot be easily converted to cash to cover short-term operating costs or acquisitions, which is one of the main differences with business assets. Current assets, on the other hand, are supposed to be liquidated within a fiscal year or operating period.

What is the Concept of a Fixed Asset?

A fixed asset is a long-term tangible piece of property or assets that a company owns and uses to produce revenue in its operations. Within a year, fixed assets are not required to be consumed or turned into cash. Land, plant, and equipment are the most common fixed assets on the balance sheet (PP&E). Capital assets are another term for them.

Key Takeaways

· Fixed assets are products that a corporation intends to use in the long run to produce revenue, such as property or facilities.

· Land, plant, and facilities are the most common terms for fixed assets (PP&E).

· Inventory and other current assets are required to be converted to cash or used within a year.

· Intangibles and long-term investments are examples of noncurrent assets, in addition to fixed assets.

· Fixed assets are amortized, while intangibles are depreciated to account for the decrease of value when the assets are used.

What is a Fixed Asset and How Does It Work?

The assets, liabilities, and shareholders' equity of a corporation are all listed on the balance sheet statement. Assets are classified into two categories: current assets and noncurrent assets, with the latter having a longer useful life. Current assets are assets that can be turned into cash in under a year. Noncurrent assets are assets and property held by a company that cannot be turned into cash quickly. Fixed assets, intangible assets, long-term investments, and deferred charges are all examples of noncurrent assets.

A fixed asset is purchased to produce or supply goods or services, renting to third parties, or internal use. The word "fixed" means that these assets will not be depleted or sold during the accounting year. A fixed asset has a physical form and is reported as PP&E on the balance sheet.

When a business buys or sells a fixed asset, the transaction is recorded on the cash flow statement under investing activities. Purchase of fixed assets results in a cash outflow for the company, while a sale results in a cash inflow. The asset is subject to an impairment write-down if its value falls below its net book value. This means that the balance sheet valuation has been adjusted downward to reflect the fact that it is overvalued in comparison to the market value.

When a fixed asset reaches the end of its useful life, it is typically sold for salvage value, which is the asset's approximate value if broken down and sold in bits. In certain situations, the asset could become redundant and, as a result, will be disposed of without compensation. The fixed asset is written off the balance sheet in either case because it is no longer in use by the company.

Current Assets vs. Fixed Assets

On the balance sheet, both current assets and fixed assets are listed, with current assets being used or converted to cash in the short term (less than one year) and fixed assets being used over a longer period (more than one year). Cash and cash equivalents, accounts receivable, inventory, and prepaid expenditures are all examples of current assets. Current assets are not depreciated, but fixed assets are.

Noncurrent Assets vs. Fixed Assets

Noncurrent assets are fixed assets. Long-term investments and intangibles are examples of noncurrent assets. Intangible assets are long-term fixed assets that do not have a physical counterpart. Goodwill, copyrights, trademarks, and intellectual property are examples of intangible assets. Long-term investments, on the other hand, may include bond investments that are not sold or matured within a year.

Fixed Assets Advantages

Asset information aids in the preparation of reliable financial statements, market valuations, and in-depth financial analysis. These reports are used by investors and creditors to assess a company's financial health and decide whether to purchase stock or lend money to it. Since a company can use a variety of agreed methods for recording, depreciating, and disposing of its properties, investors may examine the notes to the financial statements to learn how the figures were calculated.

Fixed assets are especially relevant in capital-intensive industries like manufacturing, which require significant PP&E investments. When a company's net cash flows for the acquisition of fixed assets are consistently negative, it may be a sign that the company is expanding or investing.

Fixed Assets Examples

Buildings, electronic equipment, software, furniture, property, machinery, and vehicles are examples of fixed assets. If a company sells products, for example, the distribution trucks it owns and uses are considered fixed assets. A company parking lot is a fixed asset if it is built by a company. It's worth noting that a fixed asset doesn't have to be "fixed" in any sense of the term. Furniture and electronic equipment are examples of assets that can be transferred from one place to another.

Particular Points to Consider

As time passes, fixed assets lose value. These assets are expensed differently than other products because they generate long-term revenue. Intangible assets are amortized, while tangible assets are depreciated regularly. Annually, a portion of the cost of an asset is expensed. The asset's value declines as the amount of depreciation on the balance sheet increases. After that, the company will adopt the asset's expense to its long-term value.

The way a company depreciates an asset will cause the asset's book value—the value that appears on the balance sheet—to vary from the actual market value at which it may be sold. The value of land cannot be depreciated.

An Overview of Current vs. Noncurrent Assets

The capital of a corporation can be divided into two types: current assets and noncurrent assets. The anticipated timeline of usage is the primary differentiator between current and noncurrent properties. On the balance sheet, current and noncurrent assets are classified. Before being summed and reconciled against liabilities and equities, they appear as separate groups.

Essential Takeaways

· Current assets are those that can be turned into cash within a year.

· Noncurrent assets are those that are deemed long-term and will not be recognized in their full value for at least a year.

· Accounts receivable and inventory are examples of current assets, while land and goodwill are examples of noncurrent assets.

· Noncurrent liabilities, such as long-term debt, are financial obligations that are not due within a year.

· The primary distinction between current and noncurrent assets and liabilities, which are also reported on the balance sheet, is their usage or payment timeline.

Assets in Use

The value of all assets that can be turned into cash within a year is referred to as current assets. Since a company's current assets are used to finance ongoing activities and cover current costs, they are isolated from other resources.

Present assets include the following:

· Money and money equivalents

· Accounts payable

· Costs charged in advance

· Inventories

· Shares that can be sold.

· Assets that aren't being used right now

Long-term investments in which the maximum value will not be realized during the accounting year are known as noncurrent assets. Anything that isn't classified as current can be classified as a noncurrent asset.

Noncurrent assets include the following:

· Property

· Real estate, machinery, and facilities (PP&E)

· Patents and trademarks

· Long-term financial commitments

· Generosity

Companies spread their expenses over many years because noncurrent assets have a long useful life. This procedure aids in the avoidance of significant losses during periods of capital growth. Noncurrent assets include both fixed assets like PP&E and intangible assets like trademarks.

Particular Points to Consider

Noncurrent liabilities, on the other hand, are a company's long-term debt commitments that do not come due within a fiscal year. Noncurrent assets are resources that a business holds, while noncurrent liabilities are resources that a business borrows and must repay.

Liabilities, which are reported on a company's balance sheet, are either money owed or services that must be performed. Noncurrent liabilities, in contrast to noncurrent assets, are a company's long-term debt commitments that are not supposed to be paid off within a year.

Noncurrent liabilities include the following:

- Long-term lease commitments
- Long-term debt, such as bonds due in the future

A business may use bonds payable to raise capital or borrow money. Bonds payable are long-term credit arrangements between borrowers and lenders. Bonds are typically issued by businesses to help fund their operations or programs. When a corporation issues bonds, it agrees to pay interest and return the principal at a fixed date, which is typically more than one fiscal year after the bond is issued. Investors like to know about a company's noncurrent liabilities to see if it has too much debt compared to its cash flow.

What Are Long-Term Assets and How Do They Work?

Long-term assets are assets or other investments made by a business that would provide long-term benefits to the company. Long-term assets, also known as noncurrent assets, can include fixed assets like a company's land, plant, and facilities, as well as other assets like long-term investments or patents.

Long-term assets are listed on the balance sheet and are typically registered at the purchase price, which does not necessarily represent the asset's current value.

Long-term assets are distinguished from current assets, which can be sold, consumed, used, or exhausted within one year by normal business operations.

· Long-term assets are investments in a business that can provide long-term benefits to the company.

· Long-term assets may include tangible assets such as a company's land, plant, and facilities, as well as intangible assets such as long-term investments or a company's trademark that cannot be physically reached.

· Long-term asset changes can indicate capital investment or liquidation.

Long-Term Assets: An Overview

Long-term assets are those that have been on the balance sheet of an organization for a long time. Long-term assets may include both tangible and intangible assets, such as a company's brand or patent, which can't be touched.

While there is no specific accounting method for determining if an asset is a long-term asset, it is widely assumed that such assets must have a useful life of more than one year.

The following are some examples of long-term assets:

· Fixed assets such as land, machinery, houses, fixtures, and vehicles, which may include land, machinery, buildings, fixtures, and vehicles

· Long-term investments, such as securities, shares, and real estate, as well as investments in other businesses.

· Patents, trademarks, and customer lists

· Goodwill, which is an intangible long-term asset gained through a merger or sale.

Long-term asset changes on a company's balance sheet may indicate capital spending or liquidation. If a company wants to invest in long-term growth, it will use profits to buy more assets that will help it gain more money in the long run. Investors should be mindful, however, that certain businesses can sell long-term assets to raise cash for short-term operating expenses or to pay a debt, which may be a sign that the company is in financial trouble.

Long-Term vs. Short-Term Assets

Current and noncurrent assets are the two categories of assets that exist on the balance sheet. Both assets and holdings that are likely to be converted into cash within a year are listed as current assets on the balance sheet. Current assets are used by businesses to finance ongoing activities and cover current expenses including accounts payable. Money, inventories, and accounts receivables are examples of current assets.

Noncurrent assets are long-term assets with a useful life of more than a year and a typical lifespan of several years. Long-term investments are less liquid, which means they can't be quickly converted into cash.

Long-Term Assets Depreciation

Depreciation is an accounting practice that requires businesses to expense a portion of long-term operating assets used in the current year. It is a non-cash cost that aims to balance sales with costs in the timeframe in which they are incurred while also increasing net income.

Long-term assets include capital assets such as plant and equipment (PP&E), except the part that will be depreciated (expensed) in the current year. Long-term assets may be depreciated on a linear or accelerated timeline, allowing the corporation to claim a tax deduction. Since depreciation can distort the true value of long-term assets and their effect on a company's profitability, analysts will often look at earnings before interest, taxes, depreciation, and amortization (EBITDA) as a key factor in understanding their financial condition.

Long-Term Assets' Limitations

Long-term investments can be costly and necessitate substantial sums of money, which can deplete a company's cash or increase its debt. One drawback to evaluating a company's long-term assets is that investors will not see the gains for a long time (possibly years). Investors must put their confidence in the management team's ability to plan for the company's future and allocate resources wisely.

Earnings aren't driven entirely by long-term assets. Drug companies spend billions of dollars on R&D to develop new products, but only a small percentage of them make it to market and are profitable.

Investors should examine a company's long-term assets holistically, just as they would any other financial measure. When doing a financial analysis of a business, it's best to use a variety of financial ratios and metrics.

What Does Property, Plant, and Equipment (PP&E) Mean?

Property, plant, and equipment are long-term assets that are critical to a company's operations but are difficult to convert into cash. Property, plant, and equipment are tangible assets in the sense that they are physical and can be touched. When compared to total assets, the total value of PP&E can range from very low to very high.

Essential Takeaways

· Fixed assets, also known as property, plant, and equipment, are physical assets that a company cannot easily liquidate.

· PP&E are long-term assets that are critical to a company's operations and long-term financial health.

· PP&E purchases indicate that management believes in the company's long-term prospects and profitability.

Understanding the terms "property, plant, and equipment"

Fixed assets, also known as property, plant, and equipment, are physical assets that a corporation cannot easily liquidate or sell. PP&E is classified as noncurrent properties, which are a company's long-term investments or assets. Noncurrent properties, such as PP&E, have a useful life of more than a year, but they normally last for several years. The polar opposite of current assets is noncurrent assets. Current assets, such as inventory, are short-term assets on the balance sheet that are likely to be turned into cash within a year.

The following are examples of land, plant, and equipment:

· Equipment

· Personal computers

· Automobiles

· Home furnishings

· Structures

· Property

Formula and Calculation for PP&E

The PP&E of an organization is used by investment analysts and accountants to decide whether it is on sound financial footing and uses funds in the most productive and profitable manner possible.

To measure PP&E, multiply capital expenses by the amount of gross property, plant, and equipment reported on the balance sheet. Subtract the result from the total depreciation. When filing financial reports, most businesses will list their net PP&E on their balance sheet, so the calculation is already completed.

Putting Money Into PP&E

For investors, a business investing in PP&E is a positive sign. A fixed asset is a significant investment in the future of a business. Purchases of PP&E show that management believes in the company's long-term prospects and profitability. Physical properties of a corporation that are intended to produce economic benefits and contribute to sales for several years are referred to as PP&E. Capital investment in PP&E is also known as a PP&E investment. Capital-intensive industries or enterprises, such as PP&E, need a large number of fixed assets.

PP&E Liquidation

If PP&E is no longer in use or a corporation is having financial problems, it can be liquidated. Selling land, plant, and machinery to finance business operations is, of course, a sign that a company is having financial difficulties. It's important to remember that regardless of whether a company sold any of its land, factory, or equipment, it's highly likely that the sale resulted in a loss. Companies may also take out a floating lien on their PP&E, which means the equipment can be used as collateral for a loan.

PP&E Accounting

PP&E is reported on the balance sheet of a company's financial statements. PP&E is initially valued at its historical cost, which includes both the purchase price and the costs of taking properties to their intended use. The historical cost of buying a building for retail operations, for example, could include the purchase price, transaction costs, and any upgrades made to the building to bring it up to code.

The value of PP&E is adjusted regularly because fixed assets lose value over time due to use and depreciation. Depreciation is the method of allocating a tangible asset's expense over its useful life to account for value declines. Accumulated depreciation is the average amount of a company's cost allocated to depreciation expense over time.

Land, on the other hand, is not depreciated because it can increase in value. It is instead measured at the current market value. Per reporting period, the PP&E account balance is remeasured, and the book value is determined after accounting for historical expense and depreciation. This number appears on the balance sheet.

Noncurrent Assets vs. PP&E

Although land, plant, and equipment are noncurrent assets or long-term assets, they are not all noncurrent assets. Nonphysical properties, such as patents and copyrights, are examples of intangible assets. They are classified as noncurrent assets because they add value to a business but cannot be turned into cash within a year. Noncurrent assets include long-term investments such as bonds and notes, which are typically kept on a company's balance sheet for more than one fiscal year. Noncurrent assets are all of a company's long-term assets, whereas PP&E applies to specific fixed, tangible assets.

Property, Plant, and Equipment Limitations

Many businesses' long-term performance depends on PP&E, but they are capital-intensive. A portion of a company's assets can be sold to raise cash and increase profit or net income. As a result, it's important to keep track of a company's PP&E investments as well as any fixed asset sales.

PP&E research excludes intangible assets, such as a company's trademark, because PP&E are tangible assets. Coca-Cola's trademark and brand name, for example, are significant intangible assets. Investors would miss the true worth of Coca-Cola's properties if they just looked at the company's PP&E. PP&E is just a small part of a company's total assets. Furthermore, PP&E has little meaning as a measure for businesses with few fixed assets.

Nonmonetary Assets: What Are They?

Nonmonetary assets are objects that a corporation owns but for which a dollar value cannot be determined precisely. These are assets whose value can change dramatically over time. When nonmonetary assets wear out or become redundant, a business will need to replace them. Factory machinery and automobiles are an example of this. Nonmonetary assets are assets that exist on the balance sheet but cannot be converted into cash or cash equivalents quickly or easily.

Essential Takeaways

· A nonmonetary asset is an asset held by a corporation that lacks a definite dollar value and is difficult to convert to cash or cash equivalents.

· Nonmonetary assets are classified as either tangible or intangible assets by businesses.

· A company's land, plant, machinery, and inventory are examples of nonmonetary assets that are considered tangible.

· A company's intellectual property, such as patents, copyrights, and trademarks, are examples of nonmonetary properties that are considered intangible.

· Monetary assets, on the other hand, can be quickly transformed into cash or cash equivalents for a certain sum of money.

Nonmonetary Assets: An Overview

Nonmonetary assets are not to be confused with monetary assets. Cash and cash equivalents, such as cash on hand, bank deposits, savings accounts, accounts receivable (AR), and notes receivable are all examples of monetary assets that can be quickly transformed into a fixed or precisely determinable sum of money.

Nonmonetary assets, on the other hand, do not have a set rate at which they can be converted into cash by the firm. A company's typical nonmonetary assets include both tangible and intangible assets. Tangible assets are the most common category of assets reported on a company's balance sheet. The inventory of a business, as well as its land, plant, and equipment, are examples of tangible assets.

Intangible properties, on the other hand, are not observable. Intangible assets may be acquired or created by businesses. Copyrights, design patents, trademarks, brand awareness, and goodwill are only a few examples.

Particular Points to Consider

It's not always clear whether a given asset is monetary or nonmonetary. In such cases, the determining factor is whether the asset's value reflects a sum that can be translated into a specific amount of cash or cash equivalent in a limited period. The asset is called a monetary asset if it can easily be transformed into cash. Assets that can be quickly transformed into cash in a short period are known as liquid assets. Assets are nonmonetary if they can't be easily converted to cash or a cash equivalent in the short term.

Nonmonetary Liabilities vs. Nonmonetary Assets

Companies frequently have nonmonetary liabilities in addition to nonmonetary assets. Nonmonetary liabilities are commitments that cannot be fulfilled by cash payments, such as warranties on products sold by a corporation. Although the dollar value of such liability can be calculated, it constitutes a duty obligation rather than a financial obligation such as loan interest payments.

Disparities of Nonmonetary Assets vs. Monetary Assets

The agreed metric for quantifying a company's assets and liabilities as they are portrayed in its financial statements are dollar values. Nonmonetary assets and liabilities, on the other hand, are included in a company's balance sheet since they cannot be easily converted to cash. Nonmonetary assets include tangible assets such as patented technologies or other intellectual property as well as real estate where a company's headquarters or manufacturing plant is located. These products are undeniably valuable commodities, but their current value fluctuates over time in response to economic and market conditions and powers. Marketplace rivalry, for example, affects the dollar value of a company's inventory by causing it to alter its market price in response to price competition from other firms or to demand the company's goods. Nonmonetary assets such as inventory and production facilities are affected by general economic factors such as inflation and deflation.

A company's monetary assets can be used to finance capital investments or to cover day-to-day operating costs. Nonmonetary assets can be used by a corporation to produce sales. A business will, for example, use its warehouse and facilities to manufacture the goods it would sell to its customers.

Chapter 6

UNDERSTANDING LIABILITY

What is the Concept of a Liability?

A liability is a debt that an individual or corporation owes to another party, typically in the form of money. Liabilities are resolved over time by exchanging economic benefits such as money, goods, or services. Liabilities include loans, accounts payable, deposits, deferred revenues, bonds, guarantees, and unpaid expenses, which are all reported on the right side of the balance sheet.

In general, liability refers to an unfulfilled or unpaid duty between two parties. Financial responsibility is an obligation in accounting, but it is more characterized by prior business transactions, activities, purchases, asset or service exchanges, or something that will provide economic gain at a later date. Liabilities are classified as either short-term (due in 12 months or less) or long-term (due in more than 12 months).

Depending on the background, liabilities are referred to as current or noncurrent liabilities. A potential service owed to others, short- or long-term borrowing from banks, individuals, or other organizations, or a prior transaction that resulted in an unresolved obligation are all examples. The most common liabilities, such as accounts payable and bonds payable, are typically the highest. These two line items would appear on most corporations' balance sheets because they are part of ongoing current and long-term activities.

Explaining Liabilities

Liabilities are an important part of a business since they are used to fund operations and major expansions. They can also improve the efficiency of business transactions. When a wine supplier sells a case of wine to a restaurant, for example, it usually does not demand payment when the products are delivered. Instead, it bills the restaurant for the order, streamlining the dropoff and making payment simpler for the restaurant.

The restaurant's unpaid debt to its wine supplier is classified as a liability. The wine supplier, on the other hand, views the money owed to it as an advantage.

Some Liability Definitions

Liability, in general, refers to the state of being accountable for something, and it may refer to any amount of money or service owed to a third party. For example, tax liability may apply to a homeowner's property taxes owed to the local government or his income tax owed to the federal government. When a retailer receives sales tax from a buyer, the retailer has a sales tax liability on their books before the funds are remitted to the county, city, or state.

Liability may also apply to a company's or an individual's legal responsibility. Many companies, for example, purchase liability insurance if a client or employee sues them for negligence.

Long-Term vs. Short-Term Liabilities

Liabilities are divided into two categories: present and long-term. Debts due within one year are classified as current liabilities, while debts due for a longer period are classified as long-term liabilities. For example, if a company takes out a 15-year mortgage, it is considered a long-term liability. The mortgage payments due this year, on the other hand, are considered the current portion of long-term debt and are reported in the balance sheet's short-term liabilities column.

Analysts want to see a company's ability to cover current obligations that are due within a year with cash. Payroll costs and accounts payable, which include money owed to retailers, monthly utilities, and other related expenses, are examples of short-term liabilities. Analysts, on the other hand, want to see evidence that long-term obligations may be covered by assets generated from potential profits or funding transactions. Bonds and loans aren't the only long-term obligations that businesses face. Long-term liabilities include things like rent, deferred taxes, payroll, and pension commitments.

Liabilities and Assets: What's the Connection?

Assets are tangible and intangible items such as structures, machinery, and appliances, as well as accounts receivable, the interest owing, trademarks, and intellectual property that a corporation owns or owes to the company.

The difference between a company's liabilities and assets is its owner's or stockholders' equity. The following is how this relationship can be expressed:

Owner's Equity = Assets - Liabilities

In most cases, however, this accounting equation is presented as follows:

Liabilities + Equity = Assets

What Is the Difference Between a Liability and an Expense?

The cost of operations that a corporation incurs to produce income is referred to as an expense. Expenses are linked to sales, unlike assets and liabilities, and both are reported on a company's income statement. In a nutshell, costs are factored into net income calculations. Revenues minus expenses are the formula for calculating net profits.

For example, if a company's expenditures exceed its profits for the past three years, it may indicate a lack of financial stability because it has been losing money during that period.

Expenses and liabilities are not interchangeable terms. One appears on a company's balance sheet, while the other appears on its income statement. Expenses are a company's operating expenses; liabilities are the company's commitments and debts. Expenses can be charged in cash right away or they can be postponed, resulting in liability.

Liabilities, like most properties, are held at expense, not market value, and can be listed in any order as long as they are classified according to GAAP rules. Under current liabilities, AT&T has a reasonably high debt ratio. Other line items such as accounts payable (AP) and various potential obligations such as payroll, taxes, and recurring expenditures for an operating business have a higher proportion in smaller businesses.

Since they cover day-to-day activities, AP usually has the highest balances. Services, raw materials, office equipment, and all other goods or services for which no promissory note is given are all examples of AP. Since most businesses do not pay for products and services as they are received, AP is akin to a stack of unpaid bills.

Common Current Liabilities Examples

· Wages Payable: This is the gross amount of unpaid compensation that workers have yet to collect. This responsibility changes often because most businesses pay their workers every two weeks.

· Interest Payable: Businesses, like people, often use credit to fund the purchase of goods and services over short periods. This is the amount of interest that must be charged on short-term loan transactions.

· Dividends Payable: This is the balance owed to shareholders after a dividend has been declared by a company that has issued stock to investors and pays a dividend. Since this cycle lasts about two weeks, this obligation appears four times a year before the dividend is paid.

Current Liabilities That Aren't as Popular

· Unearned Revenues: The obligation of a corporation to supply goods and/or services at a later date without being paid in advance. If the product or service is shipped, this amount can be decreased in the future with an offsetting entry.

· Discontinued Operations Liabilities: This is a special liability that most people overlook but should be examined more closely. Companies must account for the financial effect of operations, divisions, or entities that are currently for sale or have recently been sold. This involves the financial effect of a product line that is currently being phased out or has recently been phased out.

Since most businesses do not disclose line items for particular individuals or goods, this entry focuses on the overall consequences. Since some of the equations are based on estimates, this can have a big impact.

A good example is a major technology company that launched what it thought was a game-changing product line, only to see it fail when it reached the market. This segment must account for all costs associated with R&D, promotion, and product release.

Liabilities That do not Exist Right Now

These are liabilities that are not present under noncurrent liabilities that are due to be paid in 12 months or more, as the name suggests. Returning to the AT&T example, it has more liabilities than your typical business, which may only list one or two. Long-term debt, also known as bonds payable, is usually the most significant and highest-ranking liability.

Companies of all sizes use bonds to fund a portion of their long-term activities. Bonds are simply loans from each group that buys them. As bonds are released, mature, or are called back by the issuer, this line item is constantly changing.

Common Examples of Noncurrent Liabilities

· Warranty Liability: Certain liabilities cannot be estimated because they are not as precise as AP. It is the total amount of time and resources that will be spent fixing goods after a warranty has been agreed upon. This is a typical automotive liability since most cars come with lengthy warranties that can be expensive.

· Contingent Liability Assessment: A contingent liability could arise as a result of the outcome of a potential occurrence that is unknown.

Less Common Examples of Noncurrent Liabilities

· Deferred Credits: This is a wide category that can be registered as current or noncurrent depending on the transaction's details. These credits are money that has been accumulated until it has been paid and reported on the income statement. Customer advances, deferred revenue, or a transaction in which credits are owed but not yet considered revenue are all examples of this. This item is reduced by the amount collected and becomes part of the company's revenue stream until the revenue is no longer deferred.

· Post-Employment Benefits: These are benefits that an employee or their family members can receive upon retirement. They are recorded as a long-term liability as they accrue. This accounts for one-half of the overall noncurrent debt at AT&T, second only to long-term debt. This liability should not be underestimated, particularly in light of increasingly increasing healthcare costs and deferred compensation.

· Unamortized Investment Tax Credits (UITC): This is the difference between the asset's historical expense and the sum depreciated already. The part that hasn't been amortized is a loss, but it's just a rough approximation of the asset's fair market value. This gives an observer some insight into how vigorous or cautious a company's depreciation strategies are.

Chapter 7

HOW TO INTERPRET FINANCIAL STATEMENTS

What Are Financial Statements and What Do They Mean?

Financial statements are written documents that describe a company's operations and financial performance. Government departments, accountants, companies, and others often inspect financial statements to ensure consistency and for accounting, funding, and investment purposes.

Financial statements include the following types of documents:

· Balance sheets

· Income statements

· Cash flow statements

Essential Takeaways

· Financial statements are written accounts that detail a company's operations and financial results.

·The balance sheet is a snapshot of an organization's assets, liabilities, and stockholders' equity.

·The income statement is mainly concerned with a company's profits and expenditures for a given period. When expenditures are subtracted from profits, the statement yields net income, which is a measure of a company's earnings. The cash flow statement (CFS) assesses a company's ability to produce cash to pay debts, cover operating costs, and make investments.

Using Data From Financial Statements

Financial data is used by investors and financial analysts to evaluate a company's success and make assumptions about the stock price's potential course. The annual report, which includes the firm's financial statements, is one of the most valuable sources of accurate and audited financial results.

Investors, market analysts, and creditors use financial statements to assess a company's financial health and earnings potential. The balance sheet, income statement, and statement of cash flows are the three main financial statement reports.

Balance Sheets: An Introduction

As a snapshot of time, the balance sheet shows a company's assets, liabilities, and stockholders' equity. The snapshot is taken at the end of the fiscal year, as shown by the date at the top of the balance sheet.

The balance sheet totals may have already been determined, but here's how to find them:

1. Find total assets on the period's balance sheet.
2. Add up all of the liabilities, which should be listed separately on the balance sheet. Contingent liability may or may not be included.
3. Find total shareholder equity and multiply it by total liabilities.
4. Net assets should be equal to the number of liabilities and equity.

Information From the Income Statement

The balance sheet shows how assets are funded, whether by debt or stockholders' equity, which includes retained earnings and extra paid-in capital. On the balance sheet, assets are classified in order of liquidity.

The liabilities are listed in the order in which they are expected to be paid. Short-term or current liabilities are debts that are supposed to be paid within a year, whereas long-term or noncurrent liabilities are debts that are expected to be paid for a longer period.

Inclusions in the Balance Sheet

The following are some examples of items found on a balance sheet.

· Possessions

· Cash and cash equivalents, such as Treasury bills and certificates of deposit, are liquid assets.

· Accounts receivables are the funds owed to a business by its customers for the purchase of its goods and services.

· Liabilities for inventory

· Debt, including long-term debt

· Wages payable

· Dividends payable

Equity of Shareholders

· A company's total assets minus its total liabilities equals its shareholders' equity.

· Shareholders' equity is the amount of money that would be returned to shareholders if all of the company's assets were liquidated and all of the debt was paid off.

· Retained profits are the number of net earnings that were not paid to shareholders as dividends and are part of shareholders' equity.

Statements of Income

The income statement, unlike the balance sheet, spans a period, usually a year for annual financial statements and a quarter for quarterly financial statements. Revenues, liabilities, net profits, and earnings per share are all summarized in the income statement. It normally gives you two or three years' worth of data to compare.

Calculation and Formula for the Income Statement

Revenue - Expenses = Net Income

1. Add up all of the revenue or sales for the period.
2. Add up all of the business's revenues and costs.
3. Calculate net income or benefit for the time period by subtracting total expenditures from revenue.

Information Derived From Income Statements

One of the three major financial statements used to disclose a company's financial results for a given accounting period is the income statement. The income statement, also known as the profit and loss statement or the statement of revenue and cost, reports on a company's sales and expenditures for a specific period.

The statement produces a company's profit statistic called net income after expenditures are subtracted from revenues.

Revenue Streams

The revenue generated by selling a company's goods or services is referred to as operating revenue. The manufacturing and sale of automobiles generate operating revenue for an automobile manufacturer. Operating revenue is provided by a company's core business operations.

The income generated by non-core business operations is referred to as non-operating revenue. These earnings are unrelated to the company's primary mission and can include:

- Interest paid on cash in the bank is an indication of non-operating income
- Income from a property's rental
- Income from strategic alliances, such as royalty payment receipts
- Income from a company's property's advertising show

The revenue generated by other activities is referred to as "other profits." Gains from the sale of long-term properties such as property, equipment, or a subsidiary are examples of other profits.

Various Expenses

Main expenditures are incurred as a result of the primary operation of the company generating income. Cost of goods sold (COGS); selling, general and administrative expenses (SG&A); depreciation or amortization; and research and development are all examples of expenses (R&D). Employee salaries, sales fees, and services like energy and transportation are all common expenses.

Interest paid on loans or securities are examples of secondary activity expenses. Losses incurred as a result of the sale of an asset are often accounted for as expenditures.

The income statement's primary function is to communicate information about the profitability and financial results of business operations. When comparing different times, it can be very useful in determining if sales or income is increasing. Investors will also look at how well a company's management controls costs to see whether attempts to lower the cost of revenue can result in higher profits over time.

The cash flow statement (CFS) assesses a company's ability to produce cash to pay debts, cover operating costs, and make investments. The balance sheet and income statement are complemented by the cash flow statement.

Cash Flow Statement Details

Investors may use the CFS to understand how a company's operations work, where its money comes from, and how it is spent. The CFS may also tell you whether or not a business is financially stable.

A cash flow statement cannot be calculated using a formula. Rather, it is divided into three parts, each of which reports cash flow for the different purposes for which a business uses its funds. These three CFS components are described below.

Activities of Operation

Any sources and uses of cash from running the company and selling its goods or services are included in the operational activities on the CFS. Any adjustments in cash, accounts receivable, depreciation, inventory, and accounts payable are included in cash from operations. Wages, income tax payments, interest payments, rent, and cash receipts from the sale of a good or service are all examples of these transactions.

Investing Projects

Any sources and uses of cash from a company's investments into the long-term future of the company are considered investing projects. This category includes the purchase or sale of an asset, loans made to suppliers or obtained from buyers, and any payments related to a merger or acquisition.

This segment also includes acquisitions of fixed assets such as land, plant, and equipment. In a nutshell, improvements in facilities, properties, or investments are related to the cash generated by investing.

Activities of Financing

The sources of cash from investors or banks, as well as the uses of cash charged to shareholders, are all included in cash from funding activities. Debt issuance, equity issuance, stock repurchases, loans, dividends charged, and debt repayments are all examples of financing activities.

In three main accounting operations, the cash flow statement reconciles the income statement with the balance sheet.

Chapter 8

TIME VALUE OF MONEY

How do you Calculate the Time Value of Money (TVM)?

The idea of the time value of money states that the money you have now is worth more than the money you would have in the future due to its earning potential. This basic financial concept states that if money can gain interest, any amount of money earned earlier is worth more. The term TVM is often used to refer to the current discounted value.

Understanding Money's Time Value

The time value of money is based on the premise that reasonable investors choose to earn money now rather than the same sum of money later due to money's ability to increase in value over time. Money deposited in a savings account, for example, receives a certain interest rate and is thus said to compound in value.

Essential Takeaways

· Given that money will collect compound interest, it is more valuable in the present than in the future.

· The formula for calculating the time value of money takes into account the payment now, the future value, the interest rate, and the period.

In the time value of money formula, the number of compounding cycles within each time frame is also a significant determinant.

As an example of the reasonable investor's choice, suppose you have the option of getting $10,000 now or $10,000 in two years. Most people, it's safe to say, will take the first choice. Due to the opportunity costs associated with the delay, receiving the $10,000 today has greater importance and utility to the recipient than receiving it later, despite the equivalent value at the time of disbursement. The future benefit on interest, if money is earned today and saved for two years, is one example of such opportunity costs.

The Formula for Calculating the Time Value of Money

The time value of the money formula can vary slightly depending on the specific situation. The generalized formula, for example, has additional or fewer variables in the case of annuity or perpetuity payments. The most basic TVM formula, however, takes into account the following variables:

· I = interest rate · n = number of compounding cycles per year · t = number of years · FV = Future Value of Money · PV = Present Value of Money

The formula for TVM is based on these variables:

FV = PV x [1 + I / n)] FV = PV x [(n x t) (n x t) (n x t)]

Here's an example that uses this formula:

Assume $10,000 is invested for one year at a 10% rate of return. FV = $10,000 x [1 + (10 percent / 1)] is the money's potential value. ^ $11,000 (1 x 1)

The formula can also be rearranged to find the present-day value of the future number. PV = $5,000 / [1 + (7 percent / 1)] PV = $5,000 / [1 + (7 ^ $4,673 (1 x 1)

Compounding Periods' Effect on Future Value

The number of compounding cycles has a significant impact on TVM estimates. If the number of compounding cycles is increased to quarterly, weekly, or regularly in the $10,000 example above, the ending future value calculations are:

· Compounding on a quarterly basis: FV = $10,000 x [1 + (10 percent / 4)] (4 x 1) = $11,038

· Compounding on a monthly basis: FV = $10,000 x [1 + (10 percent / 12)] (12 x 1) = $11,047

· Compounding on a regular basis: FV = $10,000 x [1 + (10 percent / 365)] (365 x 1) = $11,052

This demonstrates that TVM is affected not only by interest rate and time horizon but also by the number of times compounding calculations are performed per year.

What Is Continuous Compounding and How Does It Work?

If compound interest is measured and reinvested into an account's balance for a potentially infinite number of periods, continuous compounding is the statistical limit. The principle of continuously compounded interest is important in finance, even though it is not feasible in reality. Most interest is compounded on a monthly, quarterly, or semiannual basis, so this is an extreme case of compounding.

Continuous Compounding Formula and Calculation

Rather than measuring interest over a finite number of periods, such as annually or weekly, continuous compounding calculates interest over an infinite number of periods. Four variables are taken into account in the compound interest formula for finite periods:

· PV = the investment's present value; I = the reported interest rate; n = the number of compounding periods; t = the time in years

The formula for continuous compounding comes from the formula for an interest-bearing investment's potential value:

PV x [1 + I / n)] = Future Value (FV)

(n x t) (n x t) (n x t)

The formula for continuously compounded interest is obtained by calculating the limit of this formula as n approaches infinity (as defined by the concept of continuous compounding):

FV = PV x e I x t), where e is a mathematical constant that is roughly equal to 2.7183.

Essential Takeaways

· The majority of interest is multiplied semiannually, quarterly, or monthly.

· Continuously compounded interest means the interest is compounded and re-added to the balance indefinitely.

· The formula for calculating continuously compounded interest takes four variables into account.

· Even though it is not feasible in reality, the idea of continuously compounded interest is significant in finance.

What You Should Learn From Continuous Compounding

Continuously compounded interest, in principle, means that an investment balance is consistently collecting interest and feeding the interest back into the balance so that it, too, is earning interest.

Interest is calculated using continuous compounding, which assumes that interest can compound over an infinite number of periods. While continuous compounding is an important principle, it is not possible to measure and pay interest over an infinite number of periods in the real world. As a result, interest is usually compounded regularly, such as weekly, quarterly, or annually.

As compared to conventional compounding times, the difference in total interest received by continuous compounding is not very significant, even with very large investment amounts.

Calculating Annuity Present and Future Value

Most of us have made or received a series of fixed payments over time, such as rent or car payments, or a series of payments over some time, such as interest on a bond or certificate of deposit (CD). Annuities are the technical term for these periodic or continuing payments (not to be confused with the financial product called an annuity, though the two are related).

There are various methods for calculating the expense of making such payments, as well as their final value. Here's what you need to know about measuring an annuity's present value (PV) or potential value (FV).

Essential Takeaways

· Annuities are recurring fees, such as rent on an apartment or interest on a mortgage.

· Contributions are made at the end of each term of ordinary annuities. When annuities are due, they are paid at the start of the contract.

· The net amount of payments at a given point in time is the potential value of an annuity.

The present value is the amount of money needed right now to make such potential payments.

Annuities are divided into two categories.

Ordinary annuities and annuities due are the two most common forms of annuities in this context.

· Ordinary annuities: Payments are made (or are required) at the end of each term of an ordinary annuity. Bonds, for example, typically pay interest once every six months.

· Annuities due: Payments for an annuity due, on the other hand, are made at the start of each year. A common example is a rent, which is usually due at the beginning of each month.

Calculating an Ordinary Annuity's Future Value

Given a given interest rate, future value (FV) is a calculation of how much a series of monthly payments will be worth at some point in the future. If you intend to spend a certain amount per month or year, for example, it will calculate how much you will have accrued at a later date. The potential benefit is useful in calculating the overall cost of a loan if you make regular payments on it.

Chapter 9

IMPACT OF DEBTS ON FINANCES

Debt can have a variety of consequences in a person's life. It can harm your credit score and prohibit you from receiving credit, such as a credit card or a loan. It can also prevent you from purchasing your dream home or even renting an apartment, and it may have a huge effect on a person's mental health.

Financial worries and mental wellbeing are well-known to go hand in hand, with half of the adults in problem debt already suffering from a mental health disorder such as severe depression or anxiety. Debt concerns and constant phone calls from creditors may trigger stress which, if left unchecked, may lead to additional issues such as insomnia, excessive anxiety, muscle tension, chest pain, and irritability.

Health Consequences

Debt may have a variety of negative effects on one's health including sleepless nights, high blood pressure, anxiety, and the sensation of being followed by a dark cloud.

Relationship Consequences

Debt may also damage relationships, with one of every four people in debt claiming that it has had a detrimental effect on their relationship. Debt routinely causes more arguments between partners and can cause relationship breakdown due to decreased positive communication and increased mistrust and blame. Others conceal their debt from their partners, which can lead to feelings of remorse and embarrassment that can exacerbate their mental health problems..

Aperture's Assistance

At Aperture, we agree that personal and family relationships are critical to our client's ability to handle debt, which is why, as part of our extensive wellness program, we provide support and guidance to both our clients and their families. We also understand that mental health issues can impact a person's ability to prepare, make financial decisions, and adjust their spending habits. That is why we provide each client with a personalized budget plan that they can execute month after month to ensure that they do not overspend and fall into debt, regardless of their mental health.

Debt's Emotional Consequences

Whether it's "good debt" or "poor debt," any debt can have a significant emotional effect. Many of us already know this, but studies show that debt is about much more than money. Being in debt can cause a variety of emotional and psychological problems.

According to CreditCards.com, the average American has $15,950 in credit card debt and 39% of Americans bear credit card debt month to month. Meanwhile, the average college graduate owes $40,000 in student loans, with those who earned a graduate or higher degrees, changed majors, or returned to school owing even more. According to a Federal Reserve Board report, one out of every five borrowers owes $50,000 or more in student loans (and 5.6% owe more than $100,000).

When you add in car loans, mortgages, medical debt, personal loans, and other debts, it's fair to say that the majority of Americans are in debt.

Different individuals are affected by debt in various ways. There is no universal debt tolerance. While one person may be anxious about a $1,000 credit card debt, another may not have given it a second thought until his student loan and credit card balances reached $200,000.

Here are some of the most common psychological and emotional problems associated with debt, regardless of the form or amount of debt.

Anxiety and Depression

Dr. John Gathergood of the University of Nottingham looked into the connection between debt and the depression and anxiety that can accompany it. Gathergood discovered in a study that people who struggle to pay off debts and loans are more than twice as likely to suffer from a variety of mental health issues, such as depression and extreme anxiety.

Anxiety can be triggered by a variety of factors, including persistent financial worries, overwhelming feelings of helplessness with no end in sight, and hopelessness. According to the report, 29% of people with a high debt burden often suffer from extreme anxiety.

Meanwhile, a report published in the journal *Social Science & Medicine* looked at household financial debt and its impact on mental and physical health. There are no surprises here: the study also discovered that having a lot of debt is linked to having a lot of stress and depression.

Similarly, the Royal College of Psychiatrists studied the results of more than 50 academic papers over time and discovered that men and women who engaged in high-risk credit behavior were more likely to experience depressive symptoms.

The Feeling of Resentment

Debt is difficult for anyone, but it's particularly difficult when it affects your marriage, relationship, or family. As a way of coping with debt, a spouse or partner can resent the other. It's normal to blame your partner for bringing more debt into the relationship, losing a job, not making enough money, or having debt-causing spending patterns.

According to Sonya Britt, assistant professor of family studies at Kansas State University, financial disagreements are the leading predictor of divorce. The Royal College of Psychiatrists has found that large sums of debt hurt a family's mental health.

Our significant others aren't the only ones who become objects of anger. You blame your boss for underpaying you or failing to give you a raise. You hate family or friends who are financially reliant on you or who are otherwise affecting your financial well-being. If you're a recent college graduate, you can begin to blame counselors and parents for failing to adequately explain the consequences of student loans.

Many people choose to resent themselves and the decisions that led to their debt. It's not unusual to look back on a decision with regret, whether it was wasteful spending, skipping health insurance, making a bad career choice, or something else.

Denial is a State of Mind

Although some people feel debt like an albatross around their necks, others tend to block it out entirely. Despite the daily reminders and overdue notices you can get, it's very normal to be in denial about your debt. Unfortunately, even if you can fully neglect your debt, it will only provide temporary relief, if any, and will almost always result in more debt piling up.

Not opening bills and bank statements, stuffing bills and late notices in a drawer and forgetting about them, not answering the phone when you think it's a creditor, or simply preferring not to deal with the debt are all examples of denial.

Staying in denial about your debt will increase your debt in several ways. Late fees and future interest rate rises will result from not paying or coping with bills, and if you're just making minimum payments on debts with interest, the balance can still grow higher as interest accrues.

Worse, denial will help you get deeper into debt by allowing you to spend more. Debt-forming habits are hard to break, whether you're in denial about how bad your debt is or looking the other way to justify transactions you can't afford.

Debt and stress are inextricably linked. It's normal to be concerned about how you'll cope with your debt and whether you'll ever be able to get out from under it when you have a mountain of money owed to you.

Having a lot of debt will make you more stressed at work, and losing your job will be even more disastrous for your finances. And every time you have to spend money, even on small things like food or gas to get to work, it can add to your stress level.

According to a survey by the American Psychological Association, a whopping 64% of graduate students said their intense worry about debt interferes with their optimum functioning. According to an Associated Press/AOL survey, people who are in debt are more likely to experience health issues, many of which are caused by stress, anxiety, and depression. It should also come as no surprise that studies show that the higher your debt-to-asset ratio, the more likely you are to suffer from stress and depression.

Debt-related stress has an effect on more than just how we function and go about our daily lives. Stress can also detract from the positive aspects of activities that would otherwise be beneficial. According to Ryan Howell, an associate professor of psychology at San Francisco State University, debt-related stress can obliterate all satisfaction gained from spending money. So, instead of increasing your levels of happiness, splurging on a new pair of shoes, an electronic gadget, or a dinner with friends—which would normally increase your levels of happiness—causes you to experience more stress due to your debt.

Anger and Dissatisfaction

Debt is difficult to consider, regardless of our own experience with it. However, when something is out of your control, it can be particularly frustrating and infuriating.

It's one thing to have to deal with student loans to attend college and obtain a degree. You could be in debt as a result of credit card purchases that gave you pleasure, such as holidays, shopping trips, and out-of-town dinners.

Dealing with debt resulting from unfortunate occurrences such as work loss, divorce, identity theft, a family death, major home or auto repairs, or unexpected medical bills can be particularly stressful. According to a study by NerdWallet Health, 56 million adults are struggling to pay medical bills, and medical bills are the leading cause of bankruptcy in the United States.

Furthermore, the debt will act as a persistent and agonizing reminder of the negative events that led to it in the first place.

Without question, looking at a stack of bills and seeing the total debt sum will lead to regret. You may come to regret your purchases, your failure to save enough money, and other poor financial decisions.

Students who are burdened by student loan debt may look back and regret not looking for scholarships, applying for financial aid, or not fully comprehending the loans they took out when they first started school. According to studies, students with more debt have lower mental health ratings than those who do not have as much debt.

Money and material possessions are often correlated with achievement in our culture, whether we like it or not. It's understandable if you feel guilty or ashamed about your debt. You may be ashamed that you aren't making enough money, that you haven't adequately managed your finances, or that your precarious financial situation is stopping you from enjoying the life you want.

According to the American Psychological Association, many graduate students feel alienated because of the stigma of having huge student loan debt.

Debt is a taboo topic, and most people don't want their family and friends to know they're in debt. In reality, according to a CreditCard.com survey, 85% of respondents were reluctant to discuss their credit card debt. As a result of this mindset, we can continue to try to project a debt-free picture, which may lead to more debt. We'll continue to say yes to lavish nights out, buy presents for friends and family that we can't afford, and strive to keep up with others' spending habits.

Dread

You can develop a fear of the consequences that can come with debt. If you're having trouble making payments on your mortgage, you may be worried about eviction or foreclosure on your house, bankruptcy, losing your services, or having your debts collected.

You might also be concerned about losing your job or that any other unforeseen event, such as your car breaking down, would financially ruin you.

Other worries associated with debt include the fear of what will happen next, the fear of never being able to pay off your debt, and the fear of how it will affect your relationships. According to a post-doctoral study conducted at the University of Wisconsin-Madison, high debt levels led to lower marriage rates among young adults.

Relief, Independence, and Achievement

These are only a couple of the optimistic emotional consequences of debt—after it's been paid off, of course.

Burying the financial burden can also help to alleviate the negative consequences of it, such as depression and low self-esteem. "Debt freedom isn't about freedom from debt," Trent, the maker of The Simple Dollar, said. "It's worry-free living."

It can also help you feel better about yourself, both mentally and physically.

Chapter 10

NEED FOR EMERGENCY SAVINGS

If you're having trouble paying your bills or can't afford to cover unforeseen expenses, you might benefit from having an emergency fund. Experts recommend keeping a liquid fund of three to six months of living expenses on hand.

This is why: Your emergency fund protects you in the event of a financial setback, and it can also help you from falling into debt. It also gives you peace of mind if you lose your job, become unable to function due to illness, or need to cover a big car or home repair. However, there are many reasons why you should seek to increase the size of your emergency fund.

You're Attempting to Pay Off the Debt

During any financial setback, your emergency fund will help you avoid adding to your debt. An emergency fund will help you pay for unexpected expenses such as vehicle repairs or medical bills. Using your emergency fund to deal with these stressful situations and keep your mind on getting out of debt. Having a buffer for unforeseen costs makes it easier to spend extra money paying off debt and reducing the interest it earns right away.

You've Just Begun Budgeting

When you first begin budgeting, you can unintentionally overlook some of the costs that must be considered. Some of these costs will be covered by your emergency fund for the first year, and then you can add them to the budget when they arise. This may include recurring costs such as taxes, as well as other things such as gifts or company fees. Your emergency fund will assist you when you make budget adjustments. Keep track of unplanned costs and make adjustments to the budget to account for them in the future.

You Have One Income

If you only have one source of income, having a large emergency fund is critical. This will assist you in coping with a job loss or illness that prevents the primary breadwinner from functioning.

If you're a one-income family or single, your emergency fund should cover at least a year's worth of expenses. Once you've paid off your debts, you'll be able to set up a more enormous emergency fund. You may need to raise your emergency fund if you are just starting a family. If you're single, start putting money together for an emergency fund as soon as possible.

You Work for Yourself or as a Contractor

It is essential to have a substantial emergency fund in place if you are self-employed, an independent contractor, or work a job that does not enable you to receive unemployment insurance.

Additionally, if you know your contract is about to expire, you can focus on the amount of money in your emergency fund. You would also want to set aside additional funds for months when business is sluggish. Keep track of your invoices to ensure that you don't forget to pay any unpaid bills. This will save you from having to dip into your emergency fund.

Your House Is Yours

When you own a house, you will be responsible for all repairs and maintenance. While you can set aside money for remodeling and most repairs, unforeseen costs such as plumbing or air conditioning repairs may arise. Your emergency fund will help you deal with these expenses and make homeownership a little less stressful. Home repairs, as well as the replacement of an air conditioner or boiler, can be costly. Create a fund to save for these costs before they happen. Make sure you account for taxes in your budget.

You're Separated From Your Family

Traveling home can be costly, and the costs increase if you need to travel at the last minute for an emergency. In a medical emergency or a funeral, having a decent emergency fund saved up will help cover the expense of last-minute flights home or to other family members. Calculate the cost of a plane fare and other costs and begin saving, and keep in mind that last-minute reservations are often more costly.

You're Dealing With Medical Issues

Your health insurance deductible may be reached every year if you have a severe medical condition. You may either need to take regular exams that add up fast, or you may need to use up all of your sick leave and end up taking unpaid days off.

A well-funded emergency fund will assist you in dealing with these expenses and making it easier for you to get through these difficult times. You can even miss work and run out of sick pay, resulting in more severe problems. This is something that your emergency fund will help with. Keep in mind that medical conditions can be costly, and insurance providers can not pay the total amount you plan.

You're Putting Money Aside for a Specific Purpose

If you're saving for a goal like buying a house or starting a company, having an emergency job will save you from having to dig into your savings when unforeseen expenses arise. This will help you stay on track with your objectives.

While your forward progress will be slowed as you restore your emergency fund, you will be able to leave the money you are saving for yourself. This is a fantastic way to safeguard your investments. Having an emergency fund will assist you in achieving your long-term financial objectives. Consider your emergency fund as a form of protection against unexpected costs.

Putting Money Aside in case of an Emergency

Emergencies are unpredictably volatile by their very nature. They have the potential to derail your financial health if they occur. If you aren't prepared, a sudden illness or injury, an unexpected job loss, or even an unexpected home or car repair can devastate your family's day-to-day cash flow.

Although emergencies cannot always be prevented, having an emergency fund will help alleviate the financial strain of dealing with them.

What is the Concept of an Emergency Fund?

An emergency fund is a savings or bank account set aside to cover or offset the costs of an unexpected event. It should not be seen as a savings account or used to measure a long-term savings plan for college tuition, a new vehicle, or a holiday. Instead, this fund acts as a safety net that can only be used in the event of a financial crisis. Only use the emergency fund for expenditures that are immediately linked to an emergency.

How Much Money do you Set Aside?

Although the size of your emergency fund can vary based on your lifestyle, monthly expenditures, wages, and dependents, the general rule is to set aside enough money to cover three to six months of expenses. This amount can seem intimidating at first, but the aim is to save a small amount every week or two to get to that goal. You may want to change the sum based on your bill commitments, family needs, job security, and other factors.

What do you do With the Cash?

Savings for an emergency should be held in an interest-bearing bank account, such as a money market or an interest-bearing savings account, that can be accessed quickly and without penalty. The risk of putting your emergency savings in mutual funds, bonds, or other investments is that they will lose value if you need the money right away. You should keep your emergency funds in an readily available account so that you don't have to pay the early withdrawal fees that come from investing your money in a certificate of deposit (CD) or IRA retirement account.

When do you Put This Money to Good Use?

The aim is to only use your emergency fund for expenditures that are specifically connected to an unanticipated emergency. You'll know how much to save by setting a precise dollar sum that should be in that account; you'll also know how much to contribute to replenishing the account if you take money out of it. When you do have to take money from this fund, it's essential to start restoring it right away. Remember that if you begin saving now, the money you save will go a long way toward fulfilling your needs when the next disaster arises.

Chapter 11

ASSET ALLOCATION

What Is Asset Allocation and How Does It Work?

Asset allocation is an investment strategy that seeks to balance risk and reward by allocating assets in a portfolio based on a person's interests, risk tolerance, and investment horizon. Since the three major asset classes – equities, fixed income, and cash and equivalents – have different levels of risk and return, they will all behave differently over time.

The Importance of Asset Allocation

There is no one-size-fits-all method for determining the best asset allocation for each entity. However, most financial experts agree that asset allocation is one of the most critical decisions that investors make. In other words, the way assets are distributed in stocks, shares, and cash and equivalents would be the primary determinants of your investment results, not the particular securities you choose.

Investors can use different asset allocations to achieve different goals. For example, someone saving for a new car in the coming year might invest in a very conservative mix of cash, certificates of deposit, and short-term bonds. Another person saving for a long-term retirement usually invests the majority of their retirement account in stocks because they have plenty of time to ride out market swings. A person's risk tolerance is also essential. Despite a long time horizon, someone who is not comfortable investing in stocks will choose a more conservative allocation.

Asset Allocation by Age

Stocks are generally recommended for five-year or more extended holding periods. For goals that are less than a year away, cash and money market accounts are acceptable. Bonds are somewhere in the middle. In the past, financial advisors advised dividing an investor's age by 100 to decide how much money should be invested in stocks. A 40-year-old, for example, will have 60% of his money invested in stocks. Provided that the average life expectancy continues to rise, some rule variations suggest subtracting age from 110 or 120. Portfolios can usually move to a more conservative asset allocation when people reach retirement age to help protect assets that have already been accumulated.

Using Life-cycle Funds to Achieve Asset Allocation

Asset-allocation mutual funds, also known as life-cycle or target-date funds, attempt to provide investors with portfolio structures that satisfy an investor's age, risk appetite, and investment goals by allocating assets appropriately. However, proponents of this strategy argue that arriving at a structured solution for allocating portfolio assets is problematic because individual investors need unique solutions.

A target-date fund, such as the Vanguard Target Retirement 2030 Fund, is an example. As of 2018, the fund's period is 12 years before the shareholder plans to retire. As of January 31, 2018, the fund's portfolio and bond allocations were 71% and 29% respectively. The fund would gradually transition to a more cautious 50/50 mix until 2030, reflecting the individual's desire for more capital preservation and reduced risk. In subsequent years, the fund shifts to a 67% bond and 33% portfolio allocation.

Five Things to Keep in Mind When It Comes to Asset Allocation

Even the most experienced investor will become perplexed when faced with thousands of stocks, shares, and mutual funds to choose from. However, if you don't do it right, you risk jeopardizing your ability to accumulate wealth and save for retirement. So, what's the safest course of action? Instead of choosing stocks, decide what combination of stocks, shares, and mutual funds you want to invest in. Your asset allocation is the term for this.

Essential Takeaways

· Asset allocation divides assets among investment vehicles in an attempt to balance risk.

· The risk-reward tradeoff is at the heart of asset allocation.

· Don't depend solely on financial planning tools or survey papers.

· Be aware of your objectives.

· Taking advantage of compounding and the time value of capital requires time.

Asset allocation is a risk-balancing investment strategy that divides assets into significant categories such as cash, bonds, securities, real estate, and derivatives. Since each asset class has its own level of risk and return, they can behave differently over time.

For example, while the value of one asset category rises, the value of another can fall or not rise as much. Some critics see this mix as a formula for poor returns, but for most investors it's the only way to avoid a significant loss if anything goes wrong in one investment class or subclass.

Most financial experts agree that asset allocation is one of the most critical decisions that investors make. In other words, the way you allocate your assets to high- and low-risk securities, short- and long-term bonds, and cash is more important than the stocks or bonds you choose.

There is no one-size-fits-all method for determining the best asset allocation for each entity. We wouldn't be able to articulate it all in one article if there was. We may, however, highlight five points that we believe are critical when considering asset allocation.

1. Return vs. Risk

   The risk-reward tradeoff is at the heart of asset allocation. It's convenient for everyone to claim they want the best possible return, but picking the highest potential assets—stocks and derivatives—isn't the solution.

   The 1929, 1981, and 1987 stock market crashes and the more recent losses following the global financial crisis from 2007 to 2009 are all examples of periods when focusing solely on stocks with the highest potential return was not the best strategy. It's time to face the facts: every year, another investor, mutual fund, pension plan, and so on will outperform you. The ability to weigh the relationship between risk and return distinguishes greedy and return-hungry investors from good ones.

Yes, investors with a higher risk tolerance should invest in stocks more. However, you can reduce your exposure to equities if you can't stay invested in the short-term volatility of a bear market.

2. Planner Sheets and Software

   Financial planning software and survey sheets created by financial advisors or investment companies may be helpful, but you can never rely on software or a predetermined strategy. For example, some advisors use an old rule of thumb to calculate the proportion of a person's portfolio allocated to stocks: deduct the person's age from 100. To put it another way, if you're 35, you can invest 65% of your money in stocks and 35% in shares, real estate, and cash. More recent guidance suggests subtracting 110 or even 120 years from your lifespan.

   On the other hand, standard worksheets can overlook important details such as whether you are a parent, a retiree, or a spouse. These worksheets are often focused on a series of basic questions that don't capture the financial objectives.

   Remember that financial institutions prefer to lock you into a standard contract not because it is the right option for you but because it is the most convenient option for them. People may use rules of thumb and planner sheets as a rough guideline, but don't get too hung up on what they say.

3. Be Aware of Your Objectives

   We all have ambitions. You should include them in your asset-allocation strategy whether your goal is to create a large retirement fund, buy a yacht or holiday home, pay for your child's education, or simply save for a new vehicle. When deciding on the correct combination of investments, all of your objectives must be taken into account.

For example, if you want to buy a beachfront retirement condo in 20 years, you won't have to worry about short-term stock market volatility. If you have a child entering college in the next five to six years, you will want to shift your asset allocation to safer fixed-income assets. As you get closer to retirement, you will want to move to a higher percentage of fixed-income assets than equity holdings.

4. Your Best Friend Is Time

   According to the United States Department of Labor, for every 10 years you put off saving for retirement—or some other long-term goal—you must save three times as much per month to catch up.

   With more time on your hands, you can not only take advantage of compounding and the time value of assets, but you can also spend more of your portfolio on higher risk/return investments, such as stocks. A couple of bad years in the stock market will most likely be remembered as nothing more than a minor blip in 30 years.

5. Simply Do It!

It's time to put your investment strategy into action once you've determined the right combination of stocks, bonds, and other assets. The first step is to determine how your current portfolio is structured.

It's simple to see how much of your investments are in stocks versus bonds but don't forget to categorize your stocks by size—small, mid, or large-cap. You should also divide your bonds into three categories based on their maturity: short, medium, and long-term.

Mutual funds, on the other hand, may be more troublesome. The names of funds don't always tell the whole story. To find out where a fund invests your money, you'll have to dig deeper into their prospectus.

Final Thoughts

When it comes to allocating your money, there is no one-size-fits-all solution. Individual investors necessitate customized solutions. Furthermore, don't be concerned if you don't have a long-term horizon. It is never too late to begin. It's also never too late to spruce up your current portfolio. Asset allocation is a lifelong process of progression and fine-tuning, not a one-time occurrence. To put it another way, it's the polar opposite of "putting all your eggs in one basket." The primary strategy for reducing risk and potentially increasing returns is to diversify the assets across asset classes.

Spreading the investments across different asset groups is referred to as asset allocation. A combination of stocks, shares, and cash or money market securities refers to broad terms.

There are subclasses within these three classes:

· Large-cap stocks: Stocks with a market capitalization of more than $10 billion

· Mid-cap stocks: Stocks with a market capitalization of between $2 billion and $10 billion

· Companies with a market capitalization of less than $2 billion are known as small-cap stocks. Because of their lower liquidity, these stocks have a higher risk.

· Any security issued by a foreign corporation and classified on a foreign exchange is known as international security.

· Emerging markets securities are securities issued by companies based in developing countries. Due to the potential for country risk and lower liquidity, these investments have a high potential return but also a high risk.

· Fixed-income securities: These are high-priced corporate or government bonds that regularly pay a specified amount of interest or at maturity and return the principal at the end of the term. They are less volatile and risky than stocks.

· Money market: Treasury bills (T-bills) are the most popular money market investment since they are short-term investments with a maturity of one year or less.

· Real estate investment trusts (REITs): Shares in a mortgage or property pool owned by a group of investors.

Key Takeaways

· Your ideal asset allocation is a mix of investments, ranging from the riskiest to the safest, that will provide you with the total return you need over time.

· There are stocks, shares, and cash or money market securities in the mix.

· The amount of your portfolio you allocate to each is determined by your time horizon and risk tolerance.

·This isn't a once-in-a-lifetime option. Check back on your decisions now and then to see if they're still fulfilling your needs and goals.

Return and Risk Maximization

Asset allocation aims to minimize risk while achieving the expected level of return. To do this, you must understand the risk-return characteristics of different asset groups.

Equities offer the best possible return, but they also carry the most risk. Since the U.S. government sponsors treasury bills, they have the lowest risk, but they also have the lowest return.

This is how the risk-reward tradeoff works. High-risk investments are best for investors with higher risk tolerance. That is, they are willing to tolerate large price fluctuations in the market. For a long-term investment portfolio, a younger investor may expect to recover over time. A couple approaching or in retirement may not want to risk their hard-earned money.

The general rule is that an investor should gradually minimize risk exposure to retire with a sufficient amount of money in secure investments.

This is why asset allocation diversification is essential. Every investment comes with its own set of risks and market swings. Your whole portfolio is protected from the ups and downs of a single stock or class of securities, thanks to asset allocation.

As a result, while part of your portfolio may be made up of more volatile securities that you've chosen for their potential for higher returns, the rest of your portfolio is made up of more stable assets.

Choosing the Best Option for You

Because each asset class has its level of risk and return, investors should base their asset composition on their risk tolerance, investment objectives, time horizon, and available funds. All of this is crucial for investors looking to build the best portfolio possible.

High-risk, high-return options may appeal to investors with a long time horizon and larger sums to invest. Low-risk, low-return allocations may be preferred by investors with smaller sums and shorter time horizons.

Many investment firms create a series of model portfolios with different proportions of asset classes to make the asset allocation process easier for clients. Each portfolio caters to a specific level of risk tolerance among investors. These model portfolios range from conservative to aggressive.

A Portfolio of Conservative Investments

Lower-risk securities, such as fixed-income and money market securities, typically allocate a large percentage of the total in conservative model portfolios.

The main goal of a conservative portfolio is to protect your portfolio's principal value. These models are often referred to as "capital preservation portfolios" because of this.

Even if you are a conservative investor who prefers to stay away from the stock market entirely, some stock exposure can help offset inflation. The equity portion can be invested in high-quality blue-chip companies or an index fund.

A Conservative-leaning Portfolio

A moderately conservative portfolio is appropriate for investors who want to preserve the majority of their portfolio's total value while taking on some risk to protect against inflation. Within this risk level, "current income" is a common strategy. You choose securities that pay a high level of dividends or coupon payments with this strategy.

A Moderately Aggressive Portfolio

Because the asset composition is almost evenly split between fixed-income securities and equities, moderately aggressive model portfolios are often referred to as balanced portfolios. Growth and income must be balanced. Because moderately aggressive portfolios are riskier than conservative portfolios, this strategy is best suited to investors with a longer time horizon (generally more than five years) and a medium risk tolerance.

Customize Your Allocations

These model portfolios and the strategies that go with them can only serve as a rough guide. You can change the proportions to suit your specific investment requirements. The way you fine-tune the models above is determined by your future capital needs and the type of investor you are.

For example, if you enjoy researching companies and devoting time to stock picking, you will most likely divide your equities portfolio into subclasses of stocks. You can achieve a specialized risk-return potential within one segment of your portfolio by doing so.

Also, the amount of cash and money market instruments you allocate to your portfolio will be determined by the amount of liquidity and safety you require.

Suppose you need liquid investments quickly or want to keep your portfolio's current value. In that case, you should consider putting a larger portion of your investment portfolio in the money market or short-term fixed-income securities.

Investors with higher risk tolerance and no liquidity concerns will allocate a smaller portion of their portfolio to these instruments.

Taking Care of Your Portfolio

You can choose from several basic allocation strategies when deciding how to allocate your portfolio. Each takes a different approach depending on the investor's time frame, goals, and risk tolerance.

It's critical to review your portfolio regularly once it's up and running. This includes taking into account how your life and financial needs have evolved. Consider whether it's time to change the way your assets are weighted.

Even if your priorities haven't changed, you might need to rebalance your portfolio. For example, if a moderately aggressive portfolio has recently made many gains from stocks, you might consider putting some of that profit into safer money market investments.

What Is a Portfolio, Exactly?

A portfolio collects financial investments that include closed-end funds and exchange-traded funds such as stocks, bonds, commodities, cash, and cash equivalents. Stocks, bonds, and cash are commonly thought to be the foundation of a portfolio, but they don't have to be. Real estate, art, and private investments are all examples of assets found in a portfolio.

You can either hold and manage your portfolio yourself or have it managed by a money manager, financial advisor, or finance professional.

Portfolios: An Overview

The wisdom of diversification is a critical concept in portfolio management: it simply means not putting all your eggs in one basket. Diversification is a risk management strategy that involves spreading investments across various financial instruments, industries, and other categories. Its goal is to maximize profits by investing in various areas that will react differently to the same event. Diversification can be accomplished in a variety of ways. It's entirely up to you how you go about doing it. Your long-term objectives, risk tolerance, and personality all play a role in determining how to construct your portfolio.

Regardless of the asset mix in your portfolio, all portfolios should have some level of diversification and reflect the investor's risk tolerance, time horizon, and investment goals.

Taking Care of a Portfolio

An investment portfolio can be compared to a pie that has been cut into wedge-shaped pieces, each representing a different asset class and type of investment. Investors strive to build a well-diversified portfolio with an appropriate risk-return portfolio allocation for their risk tolerance. Although stocks, bonds, and cash are commonly thought of as the core building blocks of a portfolio, you can diversify your holdings by adding real estate, gold stocks, various types of bonds, paintings, and other art collectibles.

The portfolio allocation described above is for an investor with low-risk tolerance. In general, a conservative strategy invests in lower-risk securities to protect the value of a portfolio. The example shows that bonds receive 50% allocation, including high-grade corporate and government bonds and municipal bonds (munis). Blue-chip or large-cap equities could account for 20% of the stock allocation, while cash, certificates of deposit (CDs), and high-yield savings accounts could account for 30% of short-term investments.

Chapter 12

HOW TO START INVESTING IN STOCKS

Investing is a method to put money aside while you're busy with other things and have it work for you so that you can reap the full benefits of your labor in the future. Investing is a means of achieving a happy outcome. Warren Buffett, the legendary investor, defines investing as "the practice of laying out money now to receive more money later." The purpose of investing is to deposit your money into one or more types of investment vehicles in the hopes of increasing their value over time.

Let's imagine you've set aside $1,000 and are ready to dive into the world of investing. Or perhaps you only have $10 extra per week and want to start investing. We'll walk you through the steps of becoming an investor and teach you how to optimize your profits while lowering your expenses.

Key Takeaways

· Investing is defined as the act of putting money or capital into an undertaking with the hopes of making a profit or generating additional income.

· Investing, unlike spending money to buy something now, sets aside money for the future in the hopes of seeing it grow over time.

· Investing entails the risk of losing money.

· The most frequent way for beginners to obtain investment experience is to invest in the stock market.

What Kind of Investor Do You Think You Are?

Before you invest your money, you must first determine what type of investor you are. An online broker like Charles Schwab or Fidelity will ask you about your investment goals and how much risk you're ready to take on when you register a brokerage account.

Some investors want to actively manage their money's growth while others prefer to "set it and forget it." Stocks, bonds, exchange-traded funds (ETFs), index funds, and mutual funds are all available through more "conventional" internet brokers, such as the two described above.

Brokers Who Work Online

Brokers might be full-service or low-cost. As the name implies, full-service brokers provide the complete spectrum of traditional brokerage services, including financial counseling for retirement, healthcare, and all things monetary. They typically exclusively work with high-net-worth clients and demand significant fees, such as a percentage of your transactions, a percentage of the assets they manage, and occasionally a yearly membership fee. At full-service brokerages, minimum account sizes of $25,000 and higher are standard. On the other hand, traditional brokers justify their high fees by providing extensive advice tailored to your specific circumstances.

Discount brokers were once the exception, but they are now the rule. Many discount online brokers also include tools for selecting and placing your trades, as well as a set-it-and-forget-it Robo-advisory service. Online brokers have incorporated more features, such as instructional content on their websites and mobile apps, as the financial services industry has developed in the twenty-first century.

Furthermore, while some cheap brokers have no (or shallow) minimum deposit requirements, you may be subject to other restrictions, and accounts without a minimum deposit may be subject to fees. If you're thinking about investing in stocks, this is something you should think about.

Following the financial crisis of 2008, a new type of investment advisor emerged: the Robo-advisor. Betterment's Jon Stein and Eli Broverman are widely acknowledged as the pioneers in the field. Their goal was to employ technology to reduce investment expenses and streamline financial advice for investors.

Other Robo-first companies have sprung up since Betterment's inception, and even major online brokers like Charles Schwab have introduced Robo-like advisory services. 58% of Americans say they will employ Robo-advice by 2025, according to a survey by Charles Schwab. A Robo-advisor may be right for you if you want an algorithm to make financial choices for you, including tax-loss harvesting and rebalancing. And, as the success of index investing has demonstrated, if your goal is to develop long-term wealth, a Robo-advisor may be a good option.

Employer-Sponsored Investing

If you're on a limited budget, put one percent of your salary towards your company's retirement plan. The truth is, you're unlikely to notice a contribution of that size.

Contributions to work-based retirement plans are deducted from your paycheck before taxes are calculated, making the payment even less painful. Once you've become used to a one percent contribution, you might be able to increase it as you obtain annual raises. The extra contributions are unlikely to be missed. If you have a 401(k) plan at work, you may already be investing in your future with mutual fund allocations and even stock in your own company.

Minimum Account Opening Requirements

Many financial organizations require a minimum deposit. In other words, unless you deposit a specific amount of money, they will not accept your account application. Some companies won't even let you open an account with a deposit of $1,000.

It's a good idea to shop around and read broker reviews before deciding where to open an account. Minimum deposits are listed at the start of each review. Some companies may not have a minimum deposit requirement. Others will frequently reduce costs, such as trading and account administration fees, if your balance exceeds a specific threshold. Others may provide a set number of commission-free trades in exchange for opening an account.

Fees and Commissions

There is no such thing as a free lunch, as economists like to say. Even though many brokers have recently raced to reduce or eliminate trading commissions, and ETFs provide index investing to everyone who can trade with a bare-bones brokerage account, all brokers must make money from their customers in some way.

In most circumstances, your broker will charge you a commission every time you purchase or sell stock. Trading commissions start at $2 per trade and can go up to $10 for some bargain brokers. Some brokers do not charge any trade commissions, but they compensate for that in other ways. Charity organizations do not provide brokerage services.

These costs can mount up quickly and impact your profitability, depending on how frequently you trade. Stock investing can be expensive if you frequently jump in and out of positions, especially if you have a limited amount of money to invest.

A trade is an order to buy or sell shares in a single firm. If you want to buy five different stocks at once, these are considered five separate deals, and you will need to pay separately for each one.

Let's say you decide to invest $1,000 in the stocks of those five companies. To do so, you'll have to pay $50 in trading fees (if the amount is $10), which is five percent of your $1,000. After trading expenses, your account would be reduced to $950 if you invested the entire $1,000. This equates to a five percent loss before your investments have even begun to earn.

If you sell these five stocks, you'll have to pay the trade expenses again, which will be another $50. It would cost you $100 to make the round trip (buying and selling) on these five stocks, or 10% of your $1,000 initial deposit. You have lost money by just entering and departing positions if your investments do not generate enough to cover this.

Loads on Mutual Funds (Fees)

Aside from the trading fee for purchasing a mutual fund, this sort of investment has extra costs. Mutual funds are professionally managed pools of investor funds that invest in a particular market area, such as large-cap U.S. stocks.

When investing in mutual funds, an investor will be charged a variety of fees. The management expense ratio (MER), which the management team changes each year depending on the number of assets in the fund, is one of the essential fees to consider. The yearly management expense ratio varies depending on the type of fund and ranges from 0.05 percent to 0.7 percent. However, the larger the MER, the greater the impact on the fund's total performance.

When purchasing mutual funds, you may encounter several sales costs known as loads. Some are front-end loads, but no-load and back-end load funds are also available. Before you acquire a fund, be sure you understand whether it has a sales load. If you wish to avoid these fees, look for no-load and no-transaction-fee funds on your broker's list.

In comparison to stock commissions, mutual fund fees are an advantage for starting investors. This is because the costs are the same regardless of how much money you invest. As a result, you can invest as little as $50 or $100 per month in a mutual fund if you meet the minimum account opening requirements. Dollar-cost averaging (DCA) is a moniker for this strategy, and it can be an excellent method to start investing.

Diversify Your Portfolio and Lower Your Risks

In the world of investing, diversification is thought to be the only free lunch. In a word, diversifying your assets reduces the chance of a single investment's poor performance negatively impacting your overall investment return.

It's a financial jargon way of saying, "Don't put all your eggs in one basket."

The most challenging way to set up diversity of investment is through stock investing. The costs of investing in a high number of equities, as previously said, may be detrimental to the portfolio. It's impossible to create a well-diversified portfolio with a $1,000 deposit, so expect to invest in one or two firms (at most) to begin with. This will put you in greater danger.

This is where mutual funds or exchange-traded funds (ETFs) provide the most value. Both types of securities are more diversified than a single stock since they contain many equities and other investments.

Final Thoughts

Even if you are just starting and have a tiny amount of money, you can invest. It's more involved than simply choosing the suitable investment (a challenging task in and of itself), and you must be conscious of the limitations you encounter as a rookie investor.

You'll need to do some research to determine the minimum deposit requirements and then compare commissions with other brokers. It's unlikely that you'll be able to diversify your portfolio while spending a tiny amount of money on specific stocks. You'll also need to decide on a broker with whom you'd like to open an account.

Investing With a Full-service Broker or on Your Own?

When choosing an investment account, it's critical to understand the differences between advisor-based, full-service brokers and more do-it-yourself bargain brokers. Each of these sorts of brokers has its own set of benefits, but the ideal choice should be based on the investor's specific requirements.

You can buy and sell bonds, mutual funds, exchange-traded funds, and other financial products through full-service and discount brokers. The cost of commissions and fees, the account opening minimum, the services and features provided, access to investment research, and tools are all variables to consider when picking between them. When it comes to investing, the investor's choices, knowledge, and comfort level are crucial.

Brokers Who Provide a Full Range of Services

Traditional full-service brokers charge commissions and fees in exchange for their investment expertise, advice, and services. As part of the service, a range of administrative responsibilities are also provided. The brokerage business executes the trade and arranges suitable settlements once a client confirms the purchase or sale. The firm handles confirmations, statements, dividends, income accounting, and year-end tax data.

Full-service brokers typically offer other services and products that touch many aspects of their client's lives in addition to developing, monitoring, and administering investment portfolios. Personal financial planning, insurance, estate planning, retirement planning, accounting services, tax guidance, and other services fall under this category.

Higher costs, ranging from one percent to two percent of assets handled each year, are charged to the client for this full service of consultation, portfolio management, and administration. In addition, when a security is acquired or sold, full-service organizations may charge a commission fee.

The advice and services you receive should, in theory, be comprehensive and suited to your specific needs; after all, that's what you're paying for.

Full-service investment firms have existed since the dawn of modern stock markets, but they were utilized mainly by the wealthy who could afford them. They dominated the retail investment environment until the mid-1970s and 1980s when bargain brokers like Vanguard and Charles Schwab emerged, making investing more accessible to consumers of all income levels.

You can choose your stocks and bonds with cheap brokers, and you may select what your overall investing strategy should be (portfolio management). You are your own financial advisor and portfolio manager.

These brokerages may provide free instructional and research tools to assist you in making investment decisions, as well as extra assistance for a fee. The discount brokerage will continue to handle account administration, including transaction execution and settlement, confirmations and statements, and any legally necessary reports.

Although they are typically lower than those charged by full-service brokerages, discount brokers may charge commissions, often around one percent. Some of these brokers may demand higher costs in exchange for more advanced investing tools, while others may offer meager costs in exchange for fundamental investment capabilities.

Factors to Consider

Take some time to assess brokers if you decide to go the full-service route. What qualifications does a broker need to provide strategic investment advice, aside from a basic understanding of stocks and bonds? Are they a certified financial planner (CFP)?? What qualities does the broker need in terms of security selection to build an effective overall portfolio? Do they have the designation of chartered financial analyst (CFA)?

Also, keep in mind that the trading-based commission compensation structure might be perceived as having a built-in conflict of interest. Is the advice given actually in the client's best interests, or is it contaminated by the broker's need to produce revenue? Once you've decided on a broker, you should keep an eye on their performance to see if the cost is justified.

Another factor to think about is the minimum deposit necessary to start an account with each broker. Some brokers have no or very low minimums, while others want thousands of dollars. Full-service and cheap brokers have different minimums.

Full-service brokers are best for investors who want a human touch and direction and aren't comfortable making their own investing decisions. Investors that are looking for low-cost investments and love performing their own research would benefit from discount brokers.

Before making a decision, it's critical to assess the costs and benefits of each broker you're considering. The FINRA BrokerCheck website is a beautiful location to start researching different brokers' backgrounds and experiences.

Investment Types at a Basic Level

There is a limitless variety of individual investments you can make, but nearly all of them fit into one of a few groups known as "asset classes." An asset class is a group of investments that share similar features and are usually subject to the same set of financial laws.

Types of Assets

The following are the asset classes that most people are familiar with:

1. Stocks/Equities

2. Bonds/investments with a fixed rate of return
3. Cash or cash equivalents (money market funds, for example).

There are several different asset classes you might want to consider investing in at some point, including:

1. Commodities and futures such as oil and gold futures
2. Alternative investments such as real estate, foreign exchange (FX), and collectibles. You should note that alternative assets are, on average, less liquid than more traditional asset groups. Stocks, for example, are a very liquid asset, whereas a private equity transaction may require you to tie up your money for at least five to seven years.
3. SRI (Sustainable, Responsible, and Impactful) investments with a primary focus on positive social or environmental benefits

Investing in Stocks

When most people hear the phrase "investing," they generally think of buying and selling stocks in publicly traded corporations. Equity investing is a common beginner's investment.

The purchase of stock shares in a publicly listed firm gives investors an ownership stake in the company. For example, if Advent Wireless (AWI) shares are currently trading at $1.28 per share, you may purchase 100 shares for $128.00.

Companies can raise funds by selling shares to help them grow or develop.

Stock investors can buy stocks to profit from price gains, sell stocks to profit from price decreases, and buy and sell options on stocks and stock indexes. Stock dividends may potentially be a source of profit for stock investors. Dividends might be compared to collecting interest or receiving a per-share bonus from the companies you own. Dividend.com is a fantastic resource for studying and comparing dividend-paying stocks.

Exchanges such as the Vancouver Stock Exchange (VSE) and the New York Stock Exchange (NYSE) trade stocks. Stock exchanges control and facilitate stock trading.

The essential component in determining a stock price is, of course, the performance of the company. Other factors that influence stock prices are the industry's overall performance in which the firm operates, the performance of competitors, economic conditions, and government actions.

Technical or fundamental analysis is frequently used to aid stock investors in their investment decisions. (See the section on "Principles of Investing - Technical and Fundamental Analysis" for further information on technical and fundamental analysis).

Stock traders may get various free information on websites like Morningstar.com, Yahoo Finance, and Zack's Finance.

Made in the USA
Coppell, TX
31 July 2022

80718918R00079